Man-Making

MEN HELPING BOYS

ON THEIR

JOURNEY TO MANHOOD

Man-Making

MEN HELPING BOYS

ON THEIR

JOURNEY TO MANHOOD

Earl Hipp

HRD Press

Published by HRD Press, Minneapolis, MN

For information or permission to quote, contact the author via the *Man-Making Website* at man-making.com.

ISBN: 978-0-9741324-6-4
Library of Congress Control Number: 2006923277

Printed in the United States of America

Cover art by Virginia Magary and Bret Slattengren
Cover design by Dreamco.com
Layout by Patti Frazee

Dedication

To Boys: Recently, I joined thirty-five other men for a Boys-to-Men rite of passage initiation weekend. In one activity, I listened to a thirteen-year-old boy talking about his "wounds." He was small, barely four feet tall, with cleverly shorn hair and soft blue eyes. He was a boy whose energy and fighting spirit would eventually earn him the initiation name of Tiger. He described his physical scars first, and then the invisible emotional wounds from the trauma and many losses in his young life. Using every bit of his limited emotional vocabulary, Tiger described the sorrow and still-wet grief he felt because his father, an alcoholic, had committed suicide by shooting his head off. Tiger talked of his rage and confusion, feeling lost, and the unbearable void his father's death had left behind. He spoke of his loneliness and his yearning for an older man in his life.

This book is dedicated to boys like Tiger, boys who take guns to school, boys lost in gangs, and all those boys who are wandering alone in the confusing and frightening territory between boyhood and manhood. It's dedicated to the hundreds of thousands of under-male-nourished boys not lucky enough to be surrounded and supported by men who care about them.

To Men: This book is also dedicated to men. To those men who feel their masculinity is incomplete, who feel a little lost on their journey to manhood, and who haven't yet found their way to the men's hut. It's dedicated to the good men who don't realize a successful journey to mature manhood must include those ancient roles and natural man-making actions of guiding young males on their journey toward becoming a man. This book is dedicated to men who have forgotten or don't realize how much they have to offer a young male, and how desperately the adolescent boys hunger for their influence.

TABLE OF CONTENTS

ACKNOWLEDGEMENTS

It really is impossible to acknowledge all the people who helped put this book in your hands. There are just too many to thank them all. A few team members close to the top of the list are: my very patient, loving, and supportive wife, Gwen; Mark Odegard for the original cover elements; Bret Slattengren and Virginia Magary for their wonderful graphic skills; and my writing ally and sometimes coach, Scott Edelstein. This second edition of Man-Making simply would not have happened were it not for Patti Frazee and her considerable editorial, book design and graphic talents.

I also want to acknowledge:

- the men who intentionally stepped forward as man-makers in my adolescence;

- the men who might have helped me on my journey to manhood but were not willing or able to reach out;

- all the supportive men and the young males in my life today for what they continue to teach me about being a man;

- the many contributors to this book. Those who shared personal memories and feelings about their quest for manhood; and especially

- the men who *will* answer this book's call to action. I acknowledge you and honor any steps you have the courage to take in service to a boy or boys.

Most importantly, I acknowledge the many young males who hunger, in boy silence, for an older man's influence. I can see you clearly, you are amazing, and you are loved.

The Call

There is a reason this book is in your hands at this moment. In some way, however faintly, you have heard the call to help boys on their journey to manhood. In these pages you'll find everything you need to become an important man-maker in the life of a young male, and directions for setting out the path toward your mature masculinity. That adventure and the boys are waiting for you at this moment. This book *is* the answer to the call you hear. Know you *are* the man to answer this call, and *now* is the time.

> *Don't ask yourself what the world needs. Ask yourself what makes you come alive and go do that, because what the world needs is people who have come alive.*

> – Howard Thurman
> African-American mystic and activist

Man-Making

MEN HELPING BOYS

ON THEIR

JOURNEY TO MANHOOD

When will our consciences grow so tender that we will act to prevent human misery rather than avenge it?

– Eleanor Roosevelt

The world needs a man's heart.

– Joseph Jastrab
Sacred Manhood, Sacred Earth

Introduction

Why Man-Making?

The Ancient Call

For thousands of years, it was the custom. When the men of the village decided the time was right, they came in the night for the adolescent boys. It began with drums beating in the distance, softly at first, and then louder. Suddenly, the men stormed in, fearsome, masked, yelling for the boys. As the little children cried, the men wrenched the young males out of the arms of the wailing women and slipped away into the darkness with their stolen treasure. Then there was running in a pack through the dense bush, wild-eyed and breathless, as the men dragged their precious prey into the darkness. There were the sounds of heavy breathing, grunting, and crying, all surrounded by the heat of the night and the stink of male sweat. After a long march, the boys found themselves in an old and sacred male place. They were thrown into a cold, dark hut and told to wait in silence.

Eventually, it began. There were fires, strange smells, and always the pounding of drums. Around the fires, the men recited old stories, male secrets were shared, and sacred dances were taught and danced. The boys endured nakedness, cold, hunger, pain, and other trials. Ancient lessons necessary for the survival of their community were unfolded before the boys. They were required to learn masculine skills, men's language, and how to take on the responsibilities that define a man.

The men took this sacred work very seriously. They knew they were making men out of boys, and in doing so, they were shaping the future of their tribe. If the boys did not make this crossing into manhood successfully, their world would end. As a man, you know this story is true because the hunger for your place in this experience still lives on in your male bones.

In their book, *King, Warrior, Magician, Lover: Rediscovering the Archetypes of the Mature Masculine*, authors Robert Moore and Douglas Gillette sum up the consequences we all experience when men don't intentionally shape boys into men:

> *The mature masculine must be reclaimed by the modern world. Its virtual absence from technologically advanced societies has resulted in one of the more serious moral crises ever to face Western civilization ... In our world, genocide is barely noticed. Rape is used as an instrument of both pathological male self-expression and ethnic war ... We tolerate planetary pollution ... Violence is becoming the preferred solution to interpersonal disputes. In all this, we see evidence that mature masculinity, in its fullness, has all but been forgotten, and that "Boy Psychology" is prevalent.*

You wouldn't be reading this book if some part of you hadn't heard this ancient call to become a maker of men. As a man, you are made for this work. It's what men have done for centuries and must continue to do . . . because no one but men can make men out of boys.

> *"It is easier to build strong children than to repair broken men."*
>
> Frederick Douglass

My Call to Man-Making

The man-making wake-up call that changed my life happened in 1997, shortly after a Sudanese refugee named Ojulu Agote and his family arrived in the United States. My wife and I were connected with this family by the sponsoring organization that brought them to the USA. At our first meeting, I asked Ojulu how I might support him in his new world. Without a moment's hesitation, he responded with, "I want you to teach my son how to be a man in your country."

Ojulu had experienced the horrors and abuses of a refugee life, was without any material resources, and was facing a mountain of practical needs. Yet at the top of his list of what was important was finding a male elder who could guide his son toward manhood and success in this new world. From his tribal background, Ojulu knew even in the best father/son relationship, other men in the community had critically important gifts for his son. I suddenly realized Ojulu was asking me to play the role of man-maker in his son's life.

I don't remember my exact reply, but I do remember feeling embarrassed, strangely inadequate, and unsure about accepting the responsibility. My path had not included fathering children. While I was doing a pretty good job of being an uncle, until that moment I hadn't considered myself a man-maker with a critical role to play in any adolescent boy's journey into manhood. For guidance on how to respond to Ojulu's request, I asked the advice of my men friends. I also created the Man-Making Website at man-making.com, where I solicited stories and suggestions from men from around the world. I was amazed to discover, with a few exceptions, most men had responses similar to my own. While many men had ideas about what was important for an adolescent male to know, few of them could identify a clear approach for teaching an emerging male how to be a man. Many men said they had been poorly prepared for manhood, felt they didn't have much to offer boys, and few felt any responsibility to guide young males on their journey to manhood.

As I considered what I was learning in my research, I started to examine my own adolescence and found old feelings of anger and sadness. I remembered when my masculinity was emerging, the men in my family and community didn't gather around me to honor this important transition and teach me the lessons about manhood I was so hungry to learn. I can look back now and see how desperately I needed, wanted, and deserved adult male involvement and support, but it never materialized to any significant degree. I was left with the women and children to figure out manhood on my own.

Without support, nurturing, and intentional man-making by older men, I became a lost adolescent boy who mostly wandered into manhood. I became an adult male who, at his core, was unaware, unsure, and confused about what it meant to be a man. I was fully functional as men go, and not unhappy. It's just that I didn't know what I was missing.

I now realize for much of my adult life I was unconsciously searching for something I couldn't name and living with lingering internal questions about what it meant to be a MAN. I didn't know what should or could be included in the full range of my masculine potential and identity. While I did well by societal standards, I never felt I had acquired that mysterious collection of male skills, knowledge, blessings, clarity about my life's purpose, and core confidence that makes up a realized, solid, mature, and upright man. Just like so many of my peers I never definitively crossed the line into manhood, and I never learned how to be there for young males when they first heard the call to manhood.

Many of the men I spoke with, or who contributed to this book, admitted they, too, were still searching for some external acknowledgement or definitive action that confirmed they had achieved adult male status. One consequence of that condition was they felt less than qualified to become man-makers and were ignoring their naturally occurring ability and responsibility to intentionally set boys on their journey to manhood.

I think the greatest tragedy is that as men, too many of us are in some form of denial about the cost of our absence in boys' lives. We have learned how not to feel implicated when we hear about adolescent boys in trouble, having difficulty in school, being over-medicated with Ritalin, dying untimely deaths on our city streets, being imprisoned in droves, and looking for guidance in the wrong places. It's easy to ignore the fact that adolescent boys, in their often-desperate and sometimes violent actions, are actually expressing a deep need for the caring influences of man-makers. They are calling out to us, but we don't hear.

> There were no men in my "tribe" growing up. There were peers and classmates at school, and "booze-buddies" on the island where I spent holidays and weekends. A few male teachers made up most of my contact with men and they were authority figures rather than mentors. My peer group was unavailable for deep stuff and "intimacy." As teenagers in the sixties, we experienced a huge generation gap from our parents and other elders. I think most of us guys muddled our way toward manhood without any guidance from adults.
>
> David – 52

Since my wake-up call, it has become clear to me that if I can help men understand and remember an adolescent boy's need for adult male support, and provide men with some guidance on how to comfortably step into some man-making action, then the lives of both men and boys will be advanced on the journey toward a positive and mature manhood.

What Men Get

All man-making activities open up huge new vistas for the males involved. When a man finds the courage to step into some form of man-making, both men and boys learn about things they'd otherwise miss. They get to see the world through another's eyes, and become better connected across the generations. The adult male begins to experience two very different kinds of benefits. The first is the release from the costs associated with ***not*** being a man-maker. The second is the enormous collection of blessings and gifts the man receives on his journey to manhood. It's very important to understand these benefits in detail.

Relief from the Costs of Denial

I believe, whether they realize it or not, men who don't answer the call to serve young males accrue both conscious and unconscious costs. Men referred to many of these burdens and discomforts in their contributions to this book. Just some of those mentioned include:

- the subtle sense of shame that comes from ignoring the responsibility to help emerging males. Having to live with the quiet voice in your head saying, "Maybe I could have done something . . .," when they hear about lost, injured, violent, or imprisoned boys.

- being out of touch with young male energy, angst, confusion, playfulness, sexual development, physicality, technology, curiosity, music, fashion, and the chance to revisit those parts of their incomplete journey to manhood.

- the sense of isolation that comes with being disconnected across the generations. The feeling of being lost on their journey to manhood without male mentors, elders, connections to young males, or close connections to other men. As a result, men expressed problems with finding their right place in the male order of things.

- confusion about their "job description" as adult males in boys' lives, their communities, and society.

- the feelings of detachment from life in their extended family, neighborhood, and community.

- being unsure or feeling incomplete as a man. Men stated they never experienced a clear and undeniable arrival into manhood that allowed a proud confidence in their masculinity.

- feeling stuck and alone on their journey to manhood.

These are just a few of the costs that can mount up when men don't honor the man-making call from deep in their genes. This is the price men pay for ***not*** discovering and implementing their instinctual, man-making talents. This is also a description of the weight that is lifted when men step forward, in some way, in service to boys.

In going over men's responses to the research questions on the Man-Making Website (man-making.com), I was surprised and saddened to learn so many men were not aware of their innate power and potential to transform young male lives. Too many men reflected a sense of core inadequacy, deep concern, and fear about the notion of becoming man-makers. When I read those responses, I was reminded of a statement titled, "Our Deepest Fear," from the book, *A Return to Love* by Marianne Williamson. It describes the profound change I've experienced and witnessed in countless men who have found the courage to step forward on their journey to manhood by choosing to serve young males.

Our Deepest Fear

Our deepest fear is not that we are inadequate. Our deepest fear is that we are powerful beyond measure. It is our light, not our darkness that most frightens us. We ask ourselves, who am I to be brilliant, gorgeous, talented, and fabulous? Actually, who are you not to be? You are a child of God. Your playing small does not serve the world. There is nothing enlightened about shrinking so that other people won't feel insecure around you. We are all meant to shine, as children do. We were born to make manifest the glory of God that is within us. It is not just in some of us; it is in everyone. And as we let our own light shine, we unconsciously give other people permission to do the same. As we are liberated from our own fear, our presence automatically liberates others.

The Gifts from Involvement with Boys

In addition to being relieved of the costs of inaction, any form of intentional man-making activity sets in motion a shift in priorities on your journey to manhood. This evolution will begin with your very first and, possibly, brief interaction with a boy or boys. Just some of what you will very quickly begin to experience includes:

- the satisfaction of knowing you're having a direct and positive impact on boys' lives;
- the pleasure of seeing young males growing into men, physically, intellectually, spiritually, and emotionally;
- a re-connection with young male energy, their spirit of playfulness, and adolescent male angst;
- constant reminders of your own adolescence and the chance to relive/revisit many of the joys, pains, grief, victories, and challenges of that period of your life. These experiences will help you to recreate, reinvent, heal, and, very often, fill in blanks left over from your incomplete journey to manhood;

- a decline in your fear of adolescent males;

- a growing comfort with your role as a man-maker, advisor, guide, and coach for young males;

- an expansion of your male literacy through a greater understanding of, and commitment to, both boys' and men's development;

- an increased trust of men and more comfort with masculine intimacy. Because of your involvement with boys and your changing perceptions, you'll be drawn toward more personal relationships with men. Over time, you will meet and make connections with like-minded guys, and your tribe of good men will expand;

- a continual flow of opportunities to develop as a man; as this process unfolds, you will understand how young males hold the keys to an important part of your complete and mature masculine identity;

- the realization you are directly influencing the quality of life for boys, yourself, your family, your community, and the future.

I love the work we're doing! I feel like a kid and like a powerful, loving man all at the same time! Cool, or as today's kids might say, "Tight!"

Rocky – 52
Facilitator, Boys to Men initiation event

Answering the Call

In reading this book, I can guarantee you will find some comfortable action you can take to make a positive difference in a boy's life. As your knowledge, sense of responsibility to boys, and understanding of the gifts waiting for you increase, you will actually get new eyes. You'll realize boys who desperately need your attention have always been around you, but they have suddenly become more visible. You will begin to see opportunities for man-making everywhere. When that happens, you'll need to make a decision about how to answer the call you heard that put this book in your hands, and how to set out on this part of your journey to manhood.

> *The real journey of discovery*
> *is not in seeing new landscapes,*
> *but in having new eyes.*

– Marcel Proust,
French intellectual,novelist, essayist, and critic

For many men, the idea of a man-making relationship or any interaction with a young male, is new and uncertain territory. Many of the men I speak with seem to want a clear and proven map of the journey before departing. This desire is normal and understandable, and you will find a guide in this book. At this moment, however, all you really need to know is reaching out to a boy isn't about doing it *right*, but about doing what feels right to you. Each man hears a different call to this work, and his path of involvement will be unique. As you will learn, in the wide variety of man-making actions you'll be reading about, there is sure to be something that fits your degree of commitment and interests.

The very best path for you will come from listening to the call you hear, listening to your heart, listening to the boys, and remembering what is true from your own journey to manhood. You really don't need to have all the answers, a clear and defined path, or even a model to emulate. Know you can simply head out because you've heard the call and you must. For centuries, men have done just that. Set out towards uncertain goals, and by using their courage, creativity, and intuition, they did what needed to be done.

You can also trust that no matter who you are, you already possess everything you need to make a positive difference in a young male's life. Remember, *all* adolescent males, even those with intact families and loving parents, need and hunger for connection to good men. I can say with absolute certainty that at this very moment, there are young males all around you who very much want your help on their journey to manhood. Right now, there is a boy hoping and waiting for you to appear in his life.

If you think about it, wouldn't you, even today, want to have an older man show a caring and supportive interest in you? There really is very little risk and so much to gain. In the pages ahead, you'll learn all you have to do to become a man-maker is to find a way to move a little in the direction of the next young man who crosses your path. You can be sure when you do, the natural forces of masculine gravity will take care of the rest.

A Guide to Using This Book

Because men want to quickly get to the information that's important to them, here is a guide to some of the main topics you'll find in the book.

A Boy's Male Tribe – Page 17

While the father-son relationship is the most powerful man-making force on the planet, this book is not about fathering. It's about man-making by all the other men in a boy's tribe. In this section, you will be reminded that even when there is a solid and loving father-son relationship, it's critically important for a boy to have a number of other men in his male "tribe." You will be invited to remember the men who supported you as an adolescent. You'll re-learn how contact with a lot of men gives a boy a safety net of support and access to a wide variety of important masculine experiences for his journey to manhood. In this section, fathers will learn a number of ways they can support relationships between a son and adult male man-makers.

The Growing Trouble in Boyland – Page 21

This section explores a small sampling of the growing body of research pointing to serious trouble in boyland. Such challenges as living with powerful and confusing boy physiology, having problems keeping up with girls in school, boys getting in trouble in their communities, the costs of emotional miseducation, and the lack of positive adult male role models, are just some of the obstacles a boy faces on his journey to manhood. If you want to learn more about these issues and become more "boy-literate," this is the place to start. As uncomfortable as it is to read, this section of the book will likely increase your motivation to serve boys.

The Man-Making Challenge – Page 45

When it comes to showing up for young males, most men are on the sidelines. In this chapter, you will learn about some of the common concerns keeping so many men from man-making actions. Read this chapter to discover that with your hesitancy, fears, or concerns, you're not alone. You will learn how to overcome these common forms of resistance and what to do to get started. Read this section if you're not already involved in man-making in some way.

Easing Into Man-Making – Page 57

Start with this chapter if you already "get it" and want to begin doing something for boys. This chapter begins the "how to" part of the book. It will show you that no matter what your current degree of interest or commitment, there is something *every* man can do, starting today, to make a difference in a young male's life. In this chapter and those that follow you will learn about a wide variety of man-making actions and relationship possibilities. You may be surprised to learn that even when you're not consciously or directly involved with young men, you're still engaged in man-making and having impact on boys.

The First Step

You wouldn't be reading this book if you hadn't heard the call to man-making and weren't the perfect man for this work. In a real way, you have already taken your first step. I'm proud of you and I honor you for the difference you are going to make.

As you read the pages ahead, you will learn about easy and comfortable actions you can take in service to a boy or boys. As your mind and heart open, an opportunity for man-making *will* present itself, and when it does, I hope you take that next courageous step. Always remember, this call to action is simply to be the man you are, right now, and to connect with a boy or boys in some way.

Please believe you already have in your bones everything necessary to be a man-maker and to help move boys along on their journey toward manhood.

1

A Boy's Challenging World

This is our island. It's a good island. Until the grown-ups come to fetch us we'll have fun.

– Spoken by Ralph in the book,
The Lord of the Flies

In the book, *The Lord of the Flies*, by the British writer William Golding, a group of thirty boys becomes stranded on a remote and uncharted island and have to figure out how to survive in a world that is dangerous and unsuited to their most basic needs. They have to do this alone and without the benefit of adult guidance. They ultimately create a misguided and violent boy culture based on their immaturity, limited life experience, and naive assumptions about manhood and civilization. Today we'd call their creation a gang; a group of lost boys with their own values, rules, language, art, attire, male hierarchy, and rites of passage. For many boys, living in today's world is similar to life on that island. What follows is a brief description of the many challenges facing boys today.

For some reason, they think that I'm just gonna end up being that sad person they talk about, like, "I knew this kid that had the greatest talent, but he let it slip all out.

16

And now he's on the streets," or, "now he's in jail." But I
don't trust nobody, and I don't like want to put my life in
other people's hands so they can like help guide me. Not
even my mom. It's just me, and I have to do it by myself.

Al-Tran – 16

A Boy's Male Tribe

For eons, boys were raised in a male tribe. Their fathers were present and they were surrounded by their male relatives and the other
men of their village. They hunted, raised crops, built structures,
and went to war in male groups. Boys grew up in and around a
hierarchy of males of different ages, and in those structures, both
directly and indirectly they learned how to become men. Males
have this tribal way of being and learning written into their brains
and they need to be around an inter-generational group of men to
discover their right place in the male order of things.

Growing up, I wasn't part of a tribe of men and my
dad wasn't around. Now my tribe consists of my youth
pastor, my former youth pastor, my mentor Derek, my
best friend Lance, and my "group" of guys. I can talk to
any of those guys about anything because I feel totally
accepted by them. It's really cool to have a group to identify with, I don't know what I'd do without them; wait, yes
I do, I'd become depressed and attempt suicide. But I have
them and I couldn't be happier about having a group of
guys rallied around me especially in my spiritual walk.

Gino – 17

Even in the best father-son relationship, there are things a
boy can get only from his male relatives and other men. Most
men, if they are helped to remember, have memories of critically
influential men who, in addition to their fathers, gave them

gifts of support, knowledge, skills, or powerful blessings in their adolescence. These other men offer unique perspectives on life and manhood and can teach a boy skills his father may not have. Finally, having a number of men involved in a boy's life shows him a bigger picture of manhood than any one adult male can provide.

> In sixth grade, I had my first male teacher. Both in the classroom and as my sixth-grade basketball coach, he gave me encouragement to do my best. He was the first male who paid attention and verbally gave me positive reinforcement I can still remember today. My father was usually angry (when drinking) or very withdrawn and quiet.
>
> Dave – 51

However, for too many of today's adolescent males, the men who could guide them toward a successful manhood have disappeared. That's why, at its heart, this book is a call to all men to become man-makers and part of a boy's male tribe. In the pages ahead, I promise you that any man, every man, will find a way to take an action in service to boys regardless of his current level of interest or commitment. In providing a broad menu of involvement options, I am challenging teachers, neighbors, spiritual guides, youth leaders, coaches, employers, counsellors, police, other boys' parents, and any male in the community who has contact with a boy or boys, to see themselves as part of the boys' male tribe.

> *Nearly every gang member I've dealt with had inadequate or no fathering and little or no elder male mentoring.*
>
> – Michael Gurian
> *The Wonder of Boys*

What Fathers Can Do

This is not a book about fathering. Without question, fathers are potentially the most powerful man-making force on the planet. Even in the worst imaginable father/son relationship, a boy has a hunger for his father that no other man will ever satisfy. If you're a father, I honor you for having done your best for your son. However, this book is about what you and other men have to offer to all boys who are in need of positive and supportive adult male attention.

> I didn't communicate that much with my own father. But Mr. Janes was one of my first mentors. He took interest in me, and instilled in me a feeling of being and thinking like a mature man. He taught me how to take on responsibilities and how to deal with making tough decisions.
>
> After him, I started looking for other men like him. I drew out their best attributes and added them to my own character to make me the best man I could be. I'd say that the best things I learned collectively from them was to dream big and pursue it hard. They taught me how to regroup and move on and bounce back from problems. They're the ones who taught me how to be a man.
>
> Dwayne – 25

Unfortunately, today, too many boys are severely under-male-parented or don't have biological fathers present in their lives at all. According to recent census data, 25% of family households with children under eighteen are headed by a female. That means over fifteen million kids, or about 20% of kids under eighteen, do not have the benefit of an adult male in the house.

My dad has never been around. I have my mom, but I hear other people say they can do things with a dad that a mom wouldn't do. It makes me feel lonely and everything, like when other people go to the park on Father's Day. I mean not sad like I was gonna cry, but sad like left out.

Jason – 12

In order for these important gifts from other men to accumulate, a father's permission and active support are usually necessary. Strange as it may seem, that support is often hard to come by. In organizations that arrange formal mentoring relationships between men and boys, it's common knowledge that some fathers feel threatened by the presence of another man in their son's life. With these feelings cooking away beneath the surface, it's easy for a dad to unconsciously, or even intentionally, work against the relationship.

A father who understands the importance of another man's involvement in his son's life can support a man-making relationship by doing the following:

- If your son makes a positive connection to another man, try not to feel threatened or undervalued. Remember, you are irreplaceable in your son's eyes. You don't have to compete with this man; he has a very different and necessary role to play in your son's life. The man's presence is not a challenge you have to counteract, but a living gift to both you and your son.

- Overtly encourage your son's connection to the men in your community. In doing so, your actions demonstrate you're not threatened by these men and that your son has your permission to have other adult male connections. Your encouragement also says you believe other men are trustworthy and have things to offer.

- Encourage, or even ask men in your life to be involved with your adolescent son. When the time is right, include your son in activities with your men friends. Adolescent boys are hyper-alert for lessons about manhood. They will love being invited and will learn a lot just by hanging around on the edges of the adult guy activities.

- Once your son has a connection with a man, let them work through their inevitable differences. If you trust the guy, you don't need to protect your son or try to fix the problem unless there is something terribly wrong. Learning to work through feelings, issues, and differences with other men in constructive ways is an important life skill for your son to learn.

- Regularly honor the man in front of your son for his gift of commitment. Knowing how precious your son is to you, and how easy it would be for you to feel threatened, the man will appreciate your validation and support. Not only will this help the relationship, it will also be good for a boy to see men holding each other in high esteem.

If you're a father, at some point you will be presented with a chance to be a man-maker for another man's son. This is an absolutely critical role for you to play, both because that boy needs what you can uniquely offer and because of the insights and lessons waiting for you in that relationship. When you step out of your parental role and into man-making for another man's son, your understanding of, and empathy for, the men who are showing up for your son will grow considerably.

The Growing Trouble in Boyland

I'm at the coffee shop for a morning meeting and taking my order is this young male creature all dressed in black, with reddish-green hair, tattoos on both his arms, and silver bars and rings piercing his eyebrows, nose, ears, tongue, and other places I shudder to imagine. While this young man may not be the norm, he was living proof teenage boys can be colorful, creative, confusing, and sometimes flat-out frightening.

Of all the animals, the boy is the most unmanageable.

– Plato
Greek Philosopher (427 BC - 347 BC)

As they move into their teens, adolescent boys often become distant, non-communicative, restless, sexual, competitive, and sometimes unmanageable. It can be hard to accept the fact that these otherworldly beings are experiencing a normal part of their life process. It's also hard to remember that in spite of appearances, they desperately need understanding, positive attention, inclusion, compassion, and especially patient guidance from men.

Given the fact adolescent boys can be so distant, testy, and intimidating, it's somehow understandable that the general cultural response is to look the other way as they move through adolescence. It's safe to say, for most boys, our current cultural posture toward their journey to manhood is to abandon them on the roadside, to leave them alone with their quest, and just hope for the best.

Their school failure, their suicides and their violence are a call to us—parents, neighbors, friends—to be available, to listen, to mentor, and not to separate from them, regardless what we've been told is "natural" for boys.

– Aaron Kipnis
*Angry Young Men: How Parents, Teachers,
and Counselors Can Help "Bad Boys" Become Good Men*

To give you a sense of what it means to be an adolescent male today, let's briefly consider the forest of challenges they will have to negotiate if they are going to have anything close to a successful launch on their journey to manhood.

Being Driven by their Biology

I remember standing in front of the bathroom mirror and searching for the much-anticipated chest hair signaling the arrival of manhood. It was a big day when a few barely masculine hairs finally showed up. I was also looking forward to the manly act of shaving and felt enormous pride when I got permission to use my dad's electric shaver to go after the not-quite-ready-for-prime-time, soft hairs that eventually appeared on my face. The whole business of my early journey toward manhood was poorly explained and little understood, yet very eagerly anticipated. I knew something major was underway in my body, but most of my big changes came as a series of disorienting and sometimes frightening surprises.

> For the longest time I was a small kid and I got picked on a lot. When my growth spurt hit at thirteen, I went from four-and-a-half feet to five-eleven in about two years. It was fun to finally be bigger, but it was hard too. I became mean and grouchy and a bully. My clothes never fit right, I'd break things because I didn't know my own strength, I was always tripping over my own feet, I mean I was changing way too fast.
>
> Mike – 18

Today, if you put the word *adolescence* in a search engine, you get a listing of fourteen million potential information sources.

There are also lots of great books available for boys on the topic of adolescence. While helpful information is more readily available than ever before in history, reading about adolescence in a book or on the internet can't fully prepare a boy for the complicated chemical, emotional, and social challenges it brings.

Just for starters, an average adolescent male is experiencing five to seven surges of testosterone a day. That singular chemical process will increase the presence of that hormone in his body up to 800% over the course of a day. This chemical is directly responsible for new and confusing feelings of physical and sexual energy, increasing strength, and feelings of personal power. This is part of the reason young males show up so full of themselves: aggressive, restless, moody, and suddenly sexual beings.

> I don't remember exactly how old I was the first time I masturbated, ten maybe. A friend of mine had actually told me what to do, but he'd not given me many details about what would happen. I had arranged everything and was in a bathtub of hot water with the soap, and behind a locked door. Once things had commenced I felt fear (what was happening?), confusion (whoa – this is different), and enormous excitement.
>
> When I finally climaxed, I could hardly stand it. The stuff leaving my body, the incredible sensations, the release of tensions, it was all so amazing I had to try again. That evening was the beginning of a wonderful new era. I had done something very manly, had a great new toy but didn't know anything about where to go from there.
>
> Ben – 29

The flood of testosterone in the adolescent boy's body guarantees the collective embarrassments of uncontrollable erections, an uncooperative voice, hair growing everywhere, and lots of acne. In addition to these trials, a boy will also experience rapid growth in the length of his arms and legs. Having this new body often leads to a sense of awkwardness and a raft of difficulties with getting it to work. As a contributor named Steve, now in his forties, points out, it can be nightmarish to simply move through the day as an adolescent male.

> When I began 9th grade in September of 1962 I was 5′6″ tall and weighed less than 100 pounds. By the June graduation from junior high school, I had grown to 6′1″, weighing only fifteen pounds more. I recall walking into English class one day, and for no discernible reason, I just fell over. No one pushed me, I did not trip on something, as best as I can recall, I just fell over. I apparently collapsed under the weight of my growing bones. As I lay on the floor trying to disentangle myself from my own limbs, I could hear my classmates and teacher howl in laughter. Tears burned my eyes as I righted myself and slunk toward the way-too-small desk in the last row.
>
> It was a year of pain. My joints ached. I could not get enough food in my belly to stop the rumbling. Every short kid in school picked a fight with me so they could say they beat up the big guy, my brothers teased me unmercifully about my pimples, I couldn't get my dick under control, my grades sucked, and girls wouldn't be seen dead with me because I looked like a death-camp survivor.
>
> Steve – 42

While boys understand something amazing is underway, they're not likely to be talking about it because it's, well, embarrassing. You can be sure just below the surface of the bravado is a young man who is confused and nervous about all the changes he's experiencing. Inside his rapidly changing body is a boy full of questions he doesn't know how to ask, who is somewhat frightened and a little angry about it all.

Not Fitting in at School

In addition to the many biological struggles on their journey to manhood, adolescent boys have to function in a world not very well suited to their needs. It starts early in schools where boys will have to endure an educational environment whose very design and function is incompatible with how their brains are wired, their new body chemistry, their enormous restless energy, and their natural learning styles.

> I have noticed girls tend to be more organized than guys, and my school puts huge emphasis on being organized. If you aren't really organized, you can actually fail some classes. We have "notebook checks," that can be worth half your grade in some classes. They are checked randomly, and if you don't have your homework, all your notes, and it's not all in order, with a table of contents, you fail. And that's really hard for some of the guys to get used to. I don't even really understand why they make us do that, but I just grit my teeth and do it. I've also noticed some of my friends are smart guys but aren't very good at taking tests.
>
> Nat – 15

Michael Thompson, co-author of the book *Raising Cain*, says, "… in schools today boys are being treated like defective girls." Because of very different hardwiring in male and female adolescent brains, we're learning that putting boys and girls in the same classes might not be fair. Currently we're asking boys to learn in ways better suited to a girl brain, such as having an emphasis on language, sitting quietly, and speaking in turn. This can be a set-up for boys to fail, *and worse, feel like they are defective...* instead of just boys.

In school I was a little kid and I was pretty much a
loner and kept to myself. I never really got phonics and
stuff so I learned to read late. That put me behind for a
long time. I'd never read out loud. The girls would never
shut up. Like they were always talking, and reading was
easier for them.

                                        Mike – 18

In the book, *The Minds of Boys*, co-author Michael Gurian
says the costs boys are paying for this situation include lower
grades, greater discipline problems, and higher dropout rates. If
it's true the structure of the current education system is part of
the problem, the data concerning the troubling trends in boys'
lives begins to make sense: the frequency with which boys are pre-
scribed Ritalin, boys' high detention rates, young males' higher
suicide rates, and the rage some boys express with acts of seemingly inexplicable violence.

In most of their academic classes, many boys will suffer
countless embarrassments because they are in competition with
girls of the same age who are more biologically mature, emotionally developed, and more naturally verbal.

In school, the prejudice against boys and their learning style differences was always apparent to me. Over and
over I heard how smart girls were, except in math. It was
obvious to me at an early age that young girls in school
were in a special elite class. They were given special privi-
leges because of their reading skills. Every boy knew that
girls were liked more by the teachers because they acted
just like the teachers and "kissed ass."
Not only did I suffer the experiences of shame and
embarrassment as a boy in school, there was something
deeper, something that went to my core. It was an assault
on not only my academic efforts, but also the very core of
my self-esteem and potential. It was an assault on who I

was and what I could become. The wound from my early school experiences is deep. Often times there were no men around, or anyone who understood boys are just different, not "problem" learners.

Jon H. – 41

No Place in Community

In most of our communities, adolescent males are left to wander their neighborhoods or the local mall looking for a place to land. They will have a hard time finding a spot where they can hang out, maybe find something to do, and not too quickly become the objects of negative attention.

> I remember one time when I was about fifteen, a few friends and I were walking to someone's house at about 6:00 p.m., and we were pulled over by a police car driving past. Some of us had lacrosse sticks because we were going to practice the next morning, but it was obvious the police officers' first thought was that we were thugs or gangbangers going to start a fight or something. I was so surprised, because I was always such a quiet, gentle guy that has never, to this day, gotten into a serious fight, but I was stereotyped as a "little punk" because of my age and sex.

Nathan – 23

R.T. Rybak, the mayor of Minneapolis, created a juvenile crime unit in the Police Department. In the first three months of the program, the mayor proudly reported, "arrests of juvenile offenders have increased 115% and charges of juvenile offenders have increased 50% when compared to last year." This is not just a tough law enforcement initiative, however. Mayor Rybak says the long-term solution to youth crime is to attack "the core issues that put kids at risk." Towards that end, as part of the initiative, the city has increased the number of youth summer jobs, expanded youth recreation, and increased funding for aggressive outreach to the most disconnected at-risk youth to out-recruit the gangs. I love to hear the mayor of a major city say, "We can't arrest the problem of crime away. We must prevent crime by creating an environment of hope for our youth. This takes all of us stepping forward to connect youth with trusted adults and give them a sense they belong."

Because there are so few places in a community where young guys can express their growing physical energy and increasing hunger for challenge without getting in trouble, when you see a skateboard park, or a public basketball court, like moths to a lightbulb, you'll always see it teaming with young males.

> My friends and me were skateboarding to school on a major street that has both businesses and houses. The city has this stupid law that kids can't skateboard on sidewalks by houses. So this cop was watching us on our boards and he waited till we skated past the pizza parlor and were in front of a house and then he nailed us. He gave us tickets and took our skateboards. My dad had to go down to the police station to get our boards back. It really isn't fair to pick on guys just being guys like that.
>
> Gabriel – 15

By not building enough boy-relevant places, young males can call their own, or providing other forms of boy-relevant activities, many communities are sending boys the message, "there is no place for you here, you are not important to us, and your needs are your problem, not ours."

> *…male participation in community life has fallen.*
> *We need to institute a means of socializing boys so that*

they will feel a part of our society, respect social values,
and strive to become accepted as men.

– The Manhood Project
Glasgow, Scotland

Media Manhood

Adolescent boys, whether they realize it or not, are constantly looking for directions to that place called *manhood*. In the absence of direct involvement with good men, the media are shaping them in subtle, tragic, and mostly destructive ways. Watching hours of television, movies, and music videos, surfing the Internet, and playing computer and video games, young boys are bombarded with confusing and inaccurate messages about what it means to be a man. In the absence of good and involved men, young males can't help acquiring a misshapen definition of manhood as a direct result of the unfortunate messages these mediums so consistently deliver.

To be nobody but yourself, in a world, which is doing
its best, night and day, to make you everybody else, means
to fight the hardest battle which any human being can
fight, and never stop fighting.

– e. e. cummings
Poet

Just one of many organizations researching this issue is Children NOW, a national organization for people "who care about children and want to ensure they are the top public policy priority." On their website at childrennow.org, you can find their research report, Boys to Men: Entertainment Media Messages About Masculinity. Some of their findings, listed here, are quite surprising.

- Although male characters in the media displayed a range of emotional behavior, including fear, anger, grief, and pain, they rarely cried.

- Almost three-fourths of children describe males on television as violent and more than two-thirds describe men and boys on television as angry.

- One in five male characters employs some form of physical aggression to solve problems.

- Across boys' favorite media, men are closely identified with the working world and high-prestige positions, while women are identified more often with their domestic status.

- More than one-third of children say they never see television males performing domestic chores such as cooking and cleaning.

- Men of color are more likely to focus on solving problems involving family, personal, romantic, or friendship issues, while white men are consistently motivated by succeeding in work, preventing and managing disaster, and pleasing non-romantic others (e.g., family members, friends, coworkers).

- Many kids believe financial wealth is an over-represented sign of success on television, and their ideas of real-life success are underrepresented on television.

Through this role-modelling of men in the media, boys are presented with a violent, sexist, unemotional, sometimes foolish, and severely limited vision of manhood—a vision that powerfully shapes their behavior and drives their expectations of what they can do, feel, and become. It's sad so many boys are heading out on their journey toward manhood with such a poor compass and bad directions.

Children NOW points out, ". . . the media is not to blame for the troubling status of boys today, but does indeed reinforce society's notions about manliness and masculinity." They add that IF media leaders were inclined to do so, they could, ". . . broaden the images and messages that define masculinity. The media can offer excitement and adventure without violence. The media can expand the job description of 'hero.' The media can influence the life script for a generation of American boys."

How long do you think it will take today's media to accept responsibility for giving at least one "generation of American boys" a positive vision of manhood? The sad reality is that for the near future the media will remain a major player in creating boys' tragic and misshapen vision of the men they can become.

Emotional Miseducation

Influences at home, school, and in the media encourage boys to shut down their feelings of empathy, sadness, love, joy, and other key components of healthy emotional functioning. Instead, our young males learn "guy" lessons such as:

- be tough and don't ever show your fear or pain;
- play hurt, bite the bullet, wrap up the wound and keep going;
- if you can't handle your problems alone, you're a wimp;
- stand on your own two feet and fight like a man;
- and never, ever, act like a girl in any way;

In acquiring their tough-guy personas, boys will give up much of their childhood playfulness and often stop trusting other boys. As a result, boys can lose the connection to many of their closest childhood friends, increasing their feelings of loneliness and isolation. In a *Portland Press Herald* article describing the second annual Boys to Men Conference, in Portland, Oregon, staff writer Abby Zimet wrote, "They are told they must be big, tough, fast, and cool. They are told they must fit in and take charge. They are told they must find their own way from tumultuous boyhood to assured manhood, buffeted as they go by the potent, numbing messages of a blockbuster culture shaped by Bruce Willis wannabes. And they are told, whatever you do, don't cry."

Every man has a few stories about the lessons, subtle or otherwise, suggesting he put his feelings away, that his emotions were unmanly, and too much of any emotion, other than anger, would make him appear weak.

> In elementary school I wasn't small or slight or any of those things. I was maybe even tall or large, but I never felt that way. I just wasn't comfortable on the playground. I was intimidated by other boys' roughness and what I would now call macho behavior. It left me afraid and unsure. The scariest thing was that the teachers and monitors not only tolerated aggressive boy behavior, they seemed to promote it through their lack of attention to a boy who cried or a boy who was experiencing pain. They communicated the attitude to us that we should just tough it out when we were hurting. I think this is where I learned to hide my feelings, not show my feelings, and to give other boys a bit of a hard time.
>
> John – 50

When boys aren't helped to develop their emotional vocabulary, they lose contact with their inner life. The messages from so many sources encouraging boys to suppress their feelings, and a distinct absence of help to develop their emotional capacity, almost guarantee adolescent boys a life of difficulty with emotional self-awareness and problems with intimate relationships.

In his book, *Real Boys: Rescuing Our Sons from the Myths of Boyhood*, author William S. Pollack describes the lessons boys learn about limiting their emotions as "the boy code." He claims the code is the summary of unspoken rules saying boys should be independent, hide their feelings, and be tough. It leaves boys free to show anger but with little connection to a full emotional life and a severely limited emotional vocabulary. Pollack is the author of the poignant quote, "When we don't let boys cry tears, some will cry bullets."

> All aspects of boys need be celebrated, but not just for their gladiatorial qualities. We don't need better warriors, we need more warriors of the heart, boys who will follow their feelings more than following orders, boys who will value friendship and love over prestige and power. Mentors of boys need to show their vulnerability almost more than their successes. Our society would benefit greatly from lessening the need for interpersonal armor. The huge costs of boys and men carrying around this armor and constantly testing each other for weakness, is costing us all peace and serenity in our lives.
>
> Rich – 50

The absence of intentional emotional education and the presence of the boy code effectively force boys to channel all of their complicated feelings into expressions of frustration and anger, the only emotions seemingly approved for young males. This destructive training produces emotionally straitjacketed boys who become men with trouble being intimate or maintaining close and personal friendships. These emotional limitations also have other consequences. The current research described in Pollack's book clearly shows, ".... boys have remarkably fragile self-esteem, and that the rates of both depression and suicide in boys are on the rise."

> Growing up, men had always been portrayed as strong and in control. You know, "men don't cry," that sort of

stuff. Being active in sports only reinforced that concept. This made adolescence even more difficult, as I confronted scenarios that made me feel compassionate, yet I felt too embarrassed to show any emotion in public, especially in front of my peers.

Steve – 29

Boy Testing

In my early teens, my pals and I hung out near a little string of stores in our neighborhood in the same way kids today are attracted to the activity around malls. On the corner was a drug store run by an unfortunate fellow named Jake who had a nervous disorder. He was slow-moving, sweated profusely, was hard of hearing, and stuttered terribly. Given all the candy and goodies in his store, he was a perfect target for our crew of marauders. Often after school, we would mount an "attack" on his "position." Very quietly, we would sneak into his store, steal candy from a rack, and then ease out, avoiding detection, if possible. Occasionally, when he saw us, he would fly into a screaming rage and come ambling after us. The chase made the adventure more exciting, but we knew we were never in any real danger of being caught. Our clashes mostly always ended with us a half a block away from the scene of the crime feeling proud of ourselves, and Jake yelling at us from the doorway of his store.

Looking back, I'm amazed at the cruelty involved in our actions. The problem was we didn't have any place to go and nothing much to do. At the same time, we had incredible physical energy, a hunger for adventure, and a need to test our growing feelings of power. In tormenting poor Jake, we were proving our skills against an adversary, a very limited adversary, but an "enemy" nonetheless.

To put it loosely, the reason why kids are crazy is because nobody can face the responsibility of bringing them up.

– John Lennon
Singer, song writer (1940-1980)

Just like my little pack of young pals, all adolescent boys are genetically prepared for any activity that will let them compete, face challenges, solve problems, and discover the power and potential in their emerging masculinity. You can see this as they endlessly try to outdo each other on a skateboard or bike trick, shooting hoops, or mastering a battle scenario in a computer game. They are looking for their rightful place in the male hierarchy and the world around them. When this doesn't happen in a supportive and managed way, young males will create their own ways to challenge the system or act out in ways that are frightening to adults. It's this type of constant testing by boys that gets them demonized by the world around them... but they have no choice. Adolescent males are being propelled by a powerful biological chemistry that demands expression and release.

Learning about the limits to boy power needs to start early. Research by Ross Parke, director of the University of California's Center for Family Studies, and by many others, clearly indicates "rough-and-tumble play" with a father or other men in a boy's early development is how boys learn to contain their expressions of dominance and to manage their expressions of personal power. The research indicates boys who experience boisterous, physical play, and a firm, but not harsh, approach to discipline tend to be more popular in the classroom and less aggressive on the playground.

Most of my testing and adventure was as part of my rebellion against my parents and my home situation. I hung out with several guys who were doing things on the fringes of criminal activity. I would steal gas and do small things that would not land me in jail but, if caught, would have surely gotten me into some type of serious trouble. This operating on the edge created quite a rush of excitement and satisfied some lust for adventure in me. Around seventeen, my competitiveness showed up in my drag racing against other guys. This never landed me in real trouble, but a couple of times I had to speed away from the drag racing area to elude the police. Now, I am not proud of the thefts or of the rambunctiousness, but at the time, it released some of the pent-up anger and energy I had.

Jim – 34

Ideally, parents will recognize a boy's need for testing very early on, and move to quickly set firm boundaries when that behavior appears. Then, as their son grows up, they will consistently enforce limits to manage their son's testing behaviors. In addition, schools and other institutions will also have consistent limit-setting and enforcement. This will provide boys with a caring and safe container to push against as they learn the lessons of control and the limitations of their power. Sadly, that container is often flimsy or not present at all in so many boys' lives.

One teacher I had, Mr. Tellis, gave me an intellectual gift by taking me out of the classroom one day in 8th grade to "have a talk." At the time, I was a typical, adolescent, wise-assed kid who had just found smoking to be cool. When he called me out of the room, I was sure I was busted. Then he said; "If you were my kid I'd kick your ass—" But the rest of his words still ring in my ears today. "… because you are far too smart and gifted to be goofing off and messing up the way you are!" Those words turned me around. That "talk" actually got me through high school with great grades … until my family situation had me drop out. His words came back to me and inspired me to get my GED and eventually a chemical engineering degree from U of Florida.

Dave – 43

When parents, teachers, or our communities are not able to contain this wild-boy energy, big problems are guaranteed. Without limits, boys become out of control. Our typical cultural response is to wait until boy-testing has pushed everyone's buttons, and then retreat to conflict, unpleasant discipline, behavior-altering drugs, school consequences, or even law enforcement in a too-late attempt to contain or manage the behavior. Young males who don't learn how to manage their emerging sense of personal power early in their development have to face serious life consequences and, in many cases, spend time in jail before they find a solid container and a clear sense of their limits.

Boys Alone

The biggest overall challenge most adolescent boys will face is finding their way on their journey to manhood without the help of male guides. Boys have no choice about heading out on the journey because they are being driven by undeniable biological forces. When the men don't show up on time, the boys are left on their own to figure out what it means to be a man.

As adolescence ends, if there is no effective initiation or mentorship, a sad thing happens. The fire of thinking, the flaring up of creativity, the bonfires of tenderness, all begin to go out.

– Robert Bly
Poet and storyteller

For boys, the result of this isolation from men means the big questions they are facing regarding relationships, profession, sexuality, and spirituality will remain largely unanswered well into adulthood. Many of the men who contributed to my web research are *still* wrestling with questions such as:

- What does it mean to be a "man"?
- How will I know when I've become a "man"?
- Where am I to go for guidance?
- What am I to believe in?
- What is my life purpose?
- What is my place in the big picture of the world around me?
- Who am I in the context of my community and should I be involved?
- How do I conduct relationships with the women in my life?
- What must I learn to survive, prosper, and be a success in a profession?

Without answers to these questions, males will feel and be stuck in the frightening never-never land between boyhood and manhood.

> There were illusions of becoming a man when I climbed mountains and did chest-thumping types of things. But I had no real clue; I've always felt like a boy looking for shelter and permission to be a man from someone else. I suppose the closest to feeling like a man was when I had a son.
>
> Gary – 51

The Hard Data

In April 1999, I was having a pretty normal spring day. I turned on the television and heard about two boys, armed to the teeth with guns, walked into Columbine High School and calmly started shooting their teachers and fellow students. It was unimaginably horrible and, until that moment, inconceivable. It was painful to stretch my definition of boyhood to include the possibility boys could be so violent and emotionally deformed. My mind kept asking, what could possibly be so wrong in a boy's life that, without blinking, he could so easily kill his teachers and classmates? My life was turned upside down by the horror of that moment. In some irrational way, I felt responsible. I felt I had let those boys down. In that moment, I resolved to do something, but I didn't have a clue where to begin. This book was born on that day.

Thanks to dramatic news coverage, most of us are painfully aware of Columbine and too many other examples of "good" boys who have become horrifically violent. While these events are still rare, these kinds of actions are an undeniably loud signal something is terribly wrong in boyland.

> I think all boys should have a good male role model.
> I think if a teenage boy doesn't have a good adult male in
> the house, things happen, bad things. Grades go down,
> bad behavior is demonstrated, and eventually stuff like
> what happened at Columbine occurs. I guess what I am
> saying is that Dylan Klebold and Eric Harris didn't have
> the good male role models they needed. The fathers might
> have lived in the same house, but they didn't give Dylan or
> Eric the help they needed when they needed it.
>
> Justin M. – 15
> Columbine student

It's hard to come out from behind the veil of denial and realize just how many boys are lost, alone, confused, and very angry. If you're like most people, you're so flooded with media tales of boy-driven street violence, stories about boys in gangs and boys going to jail for all kinds of reasons, you don't really pay attention anymore. You may be dimly aware of issues such as the increasing difficulty teachers are having controlling young males in schools, the fact that fewer males than ever are entering college, that the police in your community are utilizing gang task forces to deal with out-of-control young males, and that angry boys continue to emerge as school shooters.

While this kind of information may float around on the edge of your consciousness, the true depth of the problem is being increasingly validated by solid research. There is a rapidly accumulating body of data about the enormous costs boys and our communities are paying because we are in denial about just how lost so many boys are on their journey to manhood.

See if you can digest the following pieces of hard data and not feel compelled to do something:

- Aaron Kipnis, in his book, *Angry Young Men: How Parents, Teachers, and Counselors Can Help "Bad Boys" Become Good Men*, reports that when both girls and boys are equally misbehaving at school, boys receive eight to ten times the reprimands that their female classmates do and their penalties are more frequent and severe. Boys are removed from classrooms and serve more detention than girls. Boys comprise 71% of all school suspensions and are expelled at even higher rates. Boys drop out of school at a rate of four-to-one over girls, receive more F's, have a lower grade point average and more grade repetitions, and far exceed girls in failing to graduate. Boys are referred to special education four-to-one over girls, they represent more than 70% of the students considered learning disabled, and make up 80% of kids sent to programs for the emotionally disturbed.

- According to Harvard psychologist William Pollack, the author of *Real Boys: Rescuing Our Sons from the Myths of Boyhood*, there are many more boys at the lowest rungs of the ladder of academic achievement than ever before. Three times more boys than girls are diagnosed with ADD/ADHD (attention deficit hyperactivity disorder), and three-quarters of children taking Ritalin are boys. While more girls attempt suicide, boys "succeed" four times more frequently than girls.

- The U.S. Drug Enforcement Administration says 10% to 12% of U.S. boys are being treated with Ritalin. Since 1990, prescriptions for this drug have increased by 500%, resulting in profits to drug companies of more than $450 million annually. No other nation is following our example and, in fact, Sweden banned methylphenidate (Ritalin) back in 1968 after reports of widespread abuse.

- A 1999 report by the national SAFE KIDS campaign reported that among children ages five to fourteen, boys account for nearly 75% of all sports-related injuries. In addition, boys are more likely than girls to suffer from multiple injuries. In "combative sports" more than 300,000 high school boys are injured, 14,000 are hospitalized, and several are killed each year. About 500,000 adolescent boys risk their mental and physical health by taking steroids to pump themselves up to an unreasonable ideal of performance beyond the natural limits of their bodies.

- James Garbarino, in his book *Lost Boys: Why Our Sons Turn Violent and How We Can Save Them*, describes statistics from the FBI which show there are about 23,000 homicides a year in the United States, and in about 10% of the cases the perpetrator is a boy under eighteen.

- The U.S. Bureau of the Census reports more than fifteen million kids, or about 20% of kids under eighteen, do not have the benefit of an adult male in the house. As the phenomenon of fatherlessness has increased, so has violence. As far back as 1965, Senator Daniel Patrick Moynihan called attention to the social dangers of raising boys without benefit of a paternal presence. He wrote in a 1965 study for the Labor Department, "A community that allows a large number of young men to grow up in broken families, dominated by women, never acquiring any stable relationship to male authority, never acquiring any rational expectations about the future—that community asks for and gets chaos." The United States today has more boys and young men locked up in juvenile institutions, jails, prisons, and mental hospitals than any other nation on earth.

It's not just in the United States that hard data about the trouble in boyland is emerging. Just one example of the global nature of this issue comes from the Australian Pathways Foundation. In its position statement, members of this group describe the challenges facing boys in Australia. They say, "Our boys are in trouble. They comprise 95% of the children currently in detention in NSW [Australia]. Within the educational system, boys are nine times more likely than girls to be in detention classes, be diagnosed with Attention Deficit Disorder, or be referred to experts for emotional and behavioral problems. Compared to girls, boys are three times more likely to die from accident, injury, or suicide. They are seven times more likely to be permanently disabled, and nine times more likely to obtain a drug conviction. The suicide rate is highest for young males in the fifteen–twenty-four age range. It is time we men began to take the transition of boys, from childhood towards a mature and creative masculinity, seriously and with care."

The growing body of research data about the trouble in boy-land is a sad description of the true personal, social, and community costs of writing this collection of boyhood trauma off to "boys will be boys."

> You know, I never had heroes—men I saw as bigger than life or even just someone I wanted to emulate. I'm not sure why. Perhaps it's because they were never right in front of me where I could see them, touch them, and really believe they existed. For me, they really DIDN'T exist, at least enough to be role models for me.
>
> Steven – 31

2

The Man-Making Challenge

In truth, for you to become a successful man-maker, it's enough to just be yourself and make some kind of connection with a boy or boys. In the pages ahead, you'll find lots of options. Being a man-maker really only requires you try on the idea that as a man, you possess everything you need for man-making work. In my research, I've learned two big lessons. First, far too many men don't have a vision of manhood that includes supporting young males. Second, there are a surprisingly large number of common fears and concerns that keep adult males from involvement with boys. If you're not already engaged in man-making, here are five steps you can take to get started on this leg of your journey to manhood:

- Understanding some of the common fears and concerns men have about becoming man-makers.

- Remembering the men who were man-makers in your life and the positive impact they had.

- Believing that without reading this book, or getting any special training, you already possess everything you need to be a successful man-maker.

- Recognizing the opportunities to serve the boys all around you.

- Finding the courage to step out on this part of *your* journey into manhood.

To help you get launched as a man-maker, let's explore each of these steps in detail.

Understanding Common Concerns

The most commonly voiced concerns that came out of my research reflected a generalized fear of not being up to the task. Many men made statements like, "I don't think I have anything to offer," or "because no one was there for me, I wouldn't know what to do." Some men felt that because of their perceived personal deficiencies, they would be failures at man-making and, even worse, the boy or boys they were trying to help would be damaged in some way.

> Yes, there is hesitation when it comes to getting involved with a boy again. The biggest thing is my fear of falling short of expectations, of failing the child in some way. As a divorced father, I tried as hard as I could to remain a strong influence on my son. But my phone calls and twice-monthly weekends were not nearly enough to compensate for his mother's poor influence and that of his peer group. I was failing him, and I was losing him. I had to live with the realization you can only do so much and it might not be enough. Maybe for some, that "little bit" is more than enough, but for me, I'd have high expectations for myself.
>
> Steve – 45

Many men stated they simply didn't know any boys, while others explained they were already living over-committed lives and didn't have the time.

I could say I didn't have enough time to be involved
with boys, but as the old adage goes, we all have twenty-
four hours a day. Perhaps my lack of involvement comes
down to values. Perhaps I simply didn't care enough to
want to get involved. A second concern was in my ability
to have a positive impact.

Tim – 43

Another set of concerns was the man/boy relationship *would*
work. There were concerns the boy may "really want to know me,"
that he'd ask difficult questions that would "stir my gut" or ask
questions "I still haven't found answers for myself." There were
fears of over-involvement, that once the relationship got started,
"… I won't be able to get out, or the boy will come to depend on
me … and need me in his life." In summary, many men expressed
fears they'd be trapped in a relationship they couldn't manage,
where they wouldn't measure up, they wouldn't have enough to
offer, and as a result, they actually might damage a boy.

Men aren't supporting boys because we have been
conditioned to believe we don't make a positive difference.
We're taught our natural expressions of masculinity are
destructive and of no good value, and we are intrinsically
non-essential, or even counter-productive to the function
of healthy community. I do support young men in my
work here in New Zealand. My constant reassurance to
them is "you are OK, you are fine being just who you are,
and the world needs your unique gifts."

Ron – 48

The concern men expressed that makes me the angriest is
the fear of "what people will think." It's a tragic statement of our
times to be living in an era when lost boys are killing themselves
and others, literally being imprisoned in droves, and suffering in a

multitude of ways from lack of male attention. Against this back-drop, if a man wants to have a positive influence on a boy's life, he has to be afraid his interest will be labeled predatory, perverted, or unnatural.

> Men don't get involved with boys as they "should" because they are too scared of being called gay or a child molester. One issue here in Australia affecting careers like teaching and organizations like boy scouts, etc. is the issue of sexuality. If you want to completely destroy a man's career just mention, "questionable sexuality" and working with children. So, men don't become teachers and scout groups are scrambling everywhere to find men as leaders because of these fears.
>
> Harvey – 44

All of these concerns men carry are common, normal, predict-able, valid, and deserving of consideration. However, you wouldn't have gotten this far into the book if you didn't have courage to face these obstacles. I promise that just ahead, you'll find out you already have or will be provided with the skills needed to become a safe, skilled, and very effective man-maker. What's important to know at this moment is that your concerns are normal, you are in good company, and many men have moved beyond these same feelings to change young male lives for the better.

> *Our doubts are traitors, and makes us lose the good*
> *we oft might win, by fearing to attempt.*
> – William Shakespeare

One way to gather up the necessary courage to become a man-maker is to remember those men who pushed through their fears and showed up as positive and supportive men during your adolescence.

Remembering What Happened

If you look hard enough at your history, you will find them. I know there was at least one special man who was a coach, loving elder, an attentive relative, teacher, or other encourager for you. He was a man who took a special interest in you. This man could clearly see your gifts and talents. When you take the time to remember that man and your relationship to him, you will be reminded of the powerful and transforming effect an older man's positive attention can have on an adolescent male.

> I was a bad, bad kid who finally ended up in boarding school in the tenth grade after nearly being thrown out of yet another school for fighting. I was a NYC street rat who, at the ripe old age of fourteen, didn't take shit from anyone. I guess you could say I was saved by a man named Bob who was the head of the boys' dorm in the boarding school I was sent to in Connecticut.
>
> Bob took the time to look through my toughness and smart-ass mouth to see a passionate kid with a huge heart who just wanted to be loved. He loved me when I was good and when I was bad. He took his time with me and he taught me to let the real me out. He taught me to cook—a lifelong passion I enjoy to this day. He taught me to love children through his love for his own children. He taught me we all come in different shapes and sizes. That these differences make the beauty of our world and not to judge people because they are one way or another but to accept people for who they are inside. He taught me many more lessons than I could ever describe.
>
> Craig – 39

For most men, the desire for support from an older male continues to be a constant background hunger long into adulthood. While it's wonderful for an older guy to get an elder blessing, for adolescent boys it's a desperate need. That's why my challenge to men is to remember. Remember the feelings, the experience of being a kid held in an older man's positive and caring attention, and the many gifts you received as a result.

> I have a vivid recollection of a man who helped me as a young man. He was a British engineer working in the U.S. as a consultant to the auto industry. He introduced me to the world of British cars, a passion I still retain over thirty years later. More importantly, he taught me valuable life lessons in the process of learning how to keep old British sports cars running. I learned about patience, craftsmanship, preventive maintenance, anticipating problems, doing things the right way, virtues that have served me well through the years.
>
> Bob – 50

Throughout this book, you'll find many stories similar to Bob's story. They are offered with the hope your memory will be stirred and that you'll be reminded of men who were guides for you on your journey toward manhood. Whether the involvement of these men was direct and intentional, or it was men you observed and "absorbed," these are men who helped you become the very good man you are today.

Trusting You Are Enough

Once you're in touch with the memory of the life-changing impact adult male influences had on your journey to manhood, you have to find a way to believe the man you are today has that same man-making potential. It's quite possible the men who helped shape and direct your young male energy were unsure of their ability to make a positive difference in your life. Yet in spite of their fears about being skilled up for the job, they just decided they would do what they could to support your journey toward manhood. There is no question that men, if their hearts are open to it, can naturally enfold, acknowledge, protect, contain, nurture, inspire, and guide young men. Really believing you can make that kind of difference in a boy's life is your next big step.

Whether or not you feel like you'd make a good role model, mentor, coach, guide, teacher, initiator, or elder, the next generation of men needs you to risk having faith in your man-making abilities. You need you to believe that lying dormant within you are instinctual abilities for guiding and shaping young men in a multitude of positive ways.

There is a man-making program called the New Zealand Big Buddy Mentoring Project (bigbuddy.org.nz). It's for fatherless boys aged 7 - 12 years old. Their goal is to match a boy with ". . . a well-screened adult male who can foster a relationship similar to that of say an uncle; a relationship we hope is for life." The Big Buddy's job description is simply to be ". . .a good man showing up every week into a boy's life, assuring him another man cares for him and giving him a model of what it means to be a man. No coaching, no psychological behaviour management, no blaming of parents. Knowing there is a man he can trust to show up and to listen will increase the boy's self-esteem, improve his relationships and give him a sense of place in the world."

Instructions to men who are going to be Big Buddies are simply to "Be yourself, and have fun with the boy, letting the boy find out what makes you a role model for him." Now, ask yourself, couldn't you do that?

Recognizing the Opportunity

The sheer number of boys in need of positive, adult male interaction and influence is frightening to me. That's why this book is a call for all men to take action in service to boys. If you can over-come your natural concerns, remember what it was like to have an older man's positive attention, and then trust you really do have what it takes to be a man-maker, the next step is to open your heart. Simply carrying the intention to have some small influence in the life of a boy will change you. Rather suddenly, you'll begin to notice boys all around you and see opportunities to act.

> After doing many years of personal growth work,
> I had a pretty good level of head and heart integration.
> Because of my efforts, I felt I had more substance, clar-
> ity of purpose, capacity to nurture, understanding of
> my boundaries, and the ability for deep listening. I also
> realized that if I didn't use these new abilities in some way
> they would eventually waste away, and move me back to
> the depression I had lived with for so long. I guess it was
> that awareness and the approach of my fortieth birthday
> that caused me to look for ways to act. That's when I
> found the Boys to Men Network. I discovered one avenue
> to becoming the man I wanted to be was to find a boy
> who needed what I had to give.
>
> Eric – 40

When you become open to the idea of being a man-maker, you'll soon begin to see the thinly disguised hunger for adult male influence in the eyes of the boys you meet. You'll begin to have feelings of sadness when you hear about another lost boy gone bad with gangs or violence for lack of positive male shepherding. You'll feel a little guilty when a group of loud, swaggering, pierced adolescent males passes you and you don't acknowledge them. Suddenly, you'll begin to see man-making opportunities waiting for you everywhere. You'll begin to see those special moments in the young male universe that are ready for positive adult male influence and see them as a call for action.

Deciding Where to Start

Absolutely *any* contact between a well-intentioned man and an adolescent male will help the young man on his journey to manhood. That means no matter what your degree of interest or level of commitment, there is an action you can take that will suit you and benefit boys around you. I've organized the chapters ahead around actions and activities based on varying levels of commitment and the time they require. They include very brief encounters, casual relationships and short term connections, time spent with groups of boys, and one-on-one relationships that can extend over months or years.

All of these forms of connection to men are necessary for a boy's successful evolution into a positive manhood. That's why you can be involved in any way, level, or degree you feel comfortable and be assured you're making an important difference in boys' lives. Let's take a quick look at the menu of options I'll be describing in more detail just ahead.

- **Easing into Man-Making** (Page 57) – If you want an easy way to get started as a man-maker, begin with this section. You'll be surprised to learn how much of an influence you can have by simply being yourself and being aware of the young males around you. There are many, almost effortless actions you can take to let boys know they are seen and acknowledged by one of the men in their "village." While these actions aren't difficult, they are important for a boy's self-esteem, and you'll like what happens to you as you make them part of your life.

- **One-to-Many Man-Making** (Page 70) – If you've decided you're willing to make at least a short-term commitment to man-making, you'll find lots of suggestions and examples in this chapter. You will learn

about the many ways a motivated man can get involved
with a group of men and boys. There are descriptions of
men who have turned their hobbies and interests into
boy-relevant activities, and a long listing of volunteer
opportunities for men who want to spend time with
groups of young guys.

• **One-on-One Man-Making** (Page 104) If you're ready for
a more personal experience, start with this chapter. You'll
learn about two types of one-on-one connections.

The first is natural or informal man-making. It's the casual
and often spontaneous relationships that more or less
happen between older men and young guys. These are
connections based on mutual affinity, they vary greatly in
their duration, and have little or no formal structure.

The second form of one-on-one connection I call
Intentional Man-Making. It's when a man decides he
wants to make a positive difference in a young man's
life and intentionally signs on, usually with a mentoring
organization, to be matched with a young guy who also
wants an older man in his life.

• **Men in Action** (Page 136) – As your boy literacy evolves,
you may be drawn to activities where you and other men
create powerful man-making events. In this chapter you'll
learn about men who are creating male community-based
activity groups, doing informal initiation ceremonies, and
producing powerful rite of passage weekends for groups
of young males. Men taking action in these ways are
making an enormous and positive difference in the lives of
young males, in the lives of men, and in the quality of life
in their communities.

Regardless of what form of man-making you choose, your experience with boys will guide you to your next step. My goal in

this section is to provide you with encouragement, permission, inspiration, and a few ideas for action. What's most important for you to know at this point is that you can do it your way, with comfortable actions, and on your own terms.

> *My bedrock thesis hasn't altered much during my*
> *ministry among you: I contend that changing men changes*
> *the world! And why do men need to change? For their*
> *very own good and for the well-being of all living entities*
> *whom we touch. When men change—soulfully and pro-*
> *phetically, internally and externally—everyone rejoices.*
>
> – Tom Owen-Towle
> *New Men—Deeper Hunger*

Stepping into Action

Because you're reading this book and becoming more informed, you are *already* doing something to improve the world for the next few generations of males. I honor and congratulate you. Whatever your degree of interest, readiness, or commitment, in the pages ahead you are guaranteed to find something you can do to turn your new intentions into action. You can draw from the many suggestions offered and the shared experience of others to create the perfect form of involvement for you.

> I think men don't help boys because they're too afraid
> of being labeled a pedophile or gay even, so they distance
> themselves. So us young guys are left out in the cold. All
> in all, it's just 'cause they're scared. Hopefully men will
> start being real men and taking charge of teaching us how
> to be men and start modeling manhood for us.
>
> Gino – 17

Once you choose the man-making action that fits your current level of interest, and then lean into your intention, masculine gravity will take care of the details. Always remember, anything you do, no matter how wonderfully imperfect, will be far better than the abandonment so many boys in your community are currently experiencing. I have a favorite quote that speaks to the power of carrying an intention to action. It has proven to be true in my life and helped me to face many frightening challenges. I hope it inspires you to move toward becoming a man-maker.

> *Until one is committed, there is hesitancy, the chance to draw back, all is ineffectiveness. Concerning all acts of initiative and creation there is one elementary truth, the ignorance of which kills countless ideas and splendid plans: that the moment one definitely commits oneself providence moves too. All sorts of things occur to help one that would never otherwise have occurred. A whole stream of events issues from the decision, rising in one's favor all manner of unforeseen incidents and meetings and material assistance which no man could have dreamed would have come his way.*
> *I learned a deep respect for one of Goethe's couplets: "Whatever you can do, or dream you can do, begin it. Boldness has genius, power, and magic in it!"*
>
> – William Hutchinson Murray
> *The Scottish Himalayan Expedition*

3

Easing Into Man-Making

If you're feeling at all tentative about becoming a man-maker, consider the following easy, low-risk, but very powerful actions that can positively change boys' lives. We'll start with the one you are already doing whether you know it or not.

Just Being You

The first man-making action requires no conscious action or commitment on your part. It's called "just being you." Right at this moment, as a man just living your life, you're most likely already having a significant impact on boys.

> I didn't receive any particular lessons about being a man, I just copied what I saw older men do and assumed that is what you do to be a man. I learned the value of being the provider and the primary man in the house from my father. I learned it was all right to drink and smoke from my father. My big lessons came from my time in prison, watching the older men who had clout. I would watch their behavior and reason it out to myself. I learned how to stand up for myself and fight off whoever I needed to. I learned being a man is to protect your family and self. These lessons were acquired on a very unconscious level, and over time, I have added my own ideas. I'm still fine-tuning my perspectives.
>
> Dwayne – 25

For a young males, men are walking encyclopedias on the topic of manhood. Even when you're not doing anything intentionally to influence young guys, they are watching you. They are evaluating your every move, measuring you, seeing the man in you, and deciding what pieces of you to take with them on their journey.

> I was/am an introvert so when I was a young man I learned a lot just by watching men. One specific instance was when I went to a pool in our small town. I watched and learned men posture; they puff up and try to intimidate. I learned there were powerful men—those who intimidated, swore, and pushed others around. Then there were the un-powerful men—those who received the wrath of the powerful.
>
> Steven – 49

Without conscious intention by the men or boys, young males are being imprinted, absorbing manhood through observation and proximity. Boys are so hungry for adult male influence, men are having impact on boys' lives without even trying.

> There was this really quiet guy in my neighborhood when I was growing up. He was always out in his garage working on a cool race car. He never said much but he was OK with a couple of young guys hanging out. You could see the pleasure and acceptance in his face when we were around. We knew we were welcome and felt safe there.
>
> It was a total "guy" place with the hot car, tools, and the smell of gas and oil. I learned about tools, that you can take things apart and put them back together, and not only could you do it and not mess up, but create something amazing. We didn't talk about anything really, and I can't say I knew him at all, but I did like being there.
>
> Snake – 50

If you were to accept the fact that boys are watching you, absorbing this subtle form of instruction and guidance, would it make you want to behave differently? If you know boys are watching you, would you be inclined to be a better role model?

If you know young males are watching, would you:

- be less inclined to rage or swear watching a sporting event?
- not yell or aggressively gesture at other drivers in traffic?
- wash your hands after taking a leak in a public restroom?
- be more overtly loving toward your spouse?
- not keep the money if someone gave you the wrong change?

If you pause just briefly to consider your actions in these or similar moments, you are experiencing an early sense of responsibility for the power of your influence in a young man's life. This is the beginning of your movement toward becoming a more conscious and intentional role model and man-maker. Make no mistake; a boy somewhere has you in his sights. Just being you, an adult male, means you're having an impact. Consider your actions and your influence for a moment. What do you want your man-making legacy to be?

> As a teacher and community organizer, I am always aware of my impact and influence on young men. I know boys are always watching, observing, thinking, and studying me. With that knowledge and understanding, I move with a definite consciousness, purpose, and intent when I'm around boys. I am very aware my words and behaviors need to be clean and direct. Even in informal situations like in my home, in my yard, from my car, in the bank, or in my son's school, as an adult male I have an important responsibility to model a positive manhood.
>
> Cris – 53

Seeing/Acknowledging/Blessing

In our communities, there are relatively few places an adolescent male can go to have his emerging masculinity noticed at all, much less feel welcomed and connected to his surroundings. He might be part of a church group, on a sports team, or part of a community enhancement project through an organization such as scouting, but these kinds of experiences are for the few, the lucky.

What is more often the case is many adolescent males feel invisible, surrounded by sources of negative attention, and they live as outsiders in their own community. They wander the neighborhoods, empty lots, shopping malls, and parks looking for those few places where they can go to express their restless and physical energy without getting in trouble. For too many young males, the sense of being outside the life of their community, disconnected, invisible, and irrelevant is enormously painful. As an adult male, there are a few simple actions you can take to ease this common form of boy isolation. Without much effort on your part, you can learn to let boys know they are indeed seen, appreciated, and connected to life in their community. Let's begin with the easiest, intentional man-making action, seeing boys.

> *Boys seek from the adult male world and its male kin-ship systems the love which says, "Your young gifts, visions, strengths, and vulnerabilities are acceptable and worthy."*
>
> – Michael Gurian
> *The Wonder of Boys*

Seeing Boys

Just like the rest of us, the young guys want and need to be seen in a positive light. Powerful examples of this desire are the masterpieces of boy art found under bridges, on freeway overpasses, on the sides of buildings, and even on the sides of trucks, trains, and other moving vehicles. In every city in the world, it's possible to see the bold, colorful, artistic, and sometimes profane graffiti that shouts, "I am here! See me! Value me!" This very public art form almost demands we take notice of the boys among us. It requires us to realize these boys have something to say and are capable of creativity, beauty, and talented expression. Adults do recognize this particular expression of boys' desire for visibility and personal expression . . . by making them a crime. When the boys are caught, they are forced to paint over their artistic statements, erasing these unique expressions of their existence in our adult world.

To help boys feel seen and valued, make it your practice to see them. Catch their quick and nervous glances in your direction and actually make brief eye contact. Give them a nod of the head, a smile of recognition, or any other gesture that tells them they have been seen, and admired, by an adult male.

You can "see" boys when you are:

- out in your neighborhood,
- doing errands,
- at the mall,
- on the bus,
- at your place of worship,
- in cafes, bookstores, and grocery stores,
- at the video store,
- in line for a movie,
- at family or sporting events.

In all these places, go out of your way to intentionally notice boys. DO NOT underestimate the power of this small and singular act. Invisibility is a horrible punishment just for being a young male. Because of our discomfort around adolescent boys, and the fact that we live in a "mind your own business" world, it can be easy to feel unsure of what to do or say to them. However, for a boy who is used to feeling invisible and disconnected, just being seen and receiving a positive gesture can be a small gift of empowerment in an otherwise very neutral or negative day.

Acknowledging Boys

Acknowledging a young guy is to go one small step beyond just seeing him. It means you actually engage him and, if possible, do it in a positive way. It takes only a little extra effort to get out from behind your own shyness and fear to say a few words. A good example of this kind of connection is found in the common greetings the guys give each other, such as, "Hey, man," "Dude," or "Hey, guys." What all these greetings have in common is the speaker sees and acknowledges the manliness of the recipient. When that statement or some other form of acknowledgement comes from an older man, it's an even bigger compliment.

> I was on my way into a supermarket. It was after work, I was dressed in slacks with a tie. Three boys were sitting on their skateboards in front of the store. They were laughing and hitting each other. As I got closer, they got quiet and stopped horsing around. I walked up to the three of them, looked them in the eyes, and said, "Skateboarding is not a crime," and kept walking in the store. They jumped up and started shaking their fists at me saying, "That's right, man, that's right." I looked back and winked at them. They smiled and went back to what they were doing.
>
> Joe – 48

You can pump your acknowledgement up by finding something about a boy or group of boys to affirm. You might compliment them on their stylish attire, interesting hair color, body markings, or even pierced body parts, all of which just happen to be elements of age-old rites of passage. The guys you encounter may have some cool piece of gear, be listening to what is (for you) unusual music, or be doing something worthy of your attention. See them, and then acknowledge their incredible uniqueness with an approving smile and a few words of praise.

> My Uncle Harold was a salty, tough, uneducated, but gentle man. From the time I was nine on, he was teaching me things. He's the man who taught me how to fish and to play horseshoes. He was always complimenting me, saying how fast I caught on to things and how I was really going to be good if I kept practicing. Uncle Harold was the personification of "manly experience" to me, so I believed if he said I was good, it must be true.
>
> Greg – 48

Hopefully, you'll be able to acknowledge young males genuinely, without the stern eyes of criticism so common from older males. Men have so often been cast as disciplinarians, protectors, and enforcers that it may actually be difficult when looking at a group of boys to not see them as "up to something" and needing to be "straightened out." It may take serious effort on your part to shift your perspective to be able to see all the things that are "right with this picture." As much as a boy or group of boys may even need a little *direction*, leave that to others. Try choosing to positively acknowledge a boy or boys and then delight in the response you get.

> As an adolescent growing up in Australia during the post World War Two years, it seemed positive attention was either nonexistent or very hard to come by. Mostly, the grown men at that time were ill equipped to dispense an appreciative comment. There was plenty of advice-

giving as a substitute, usually in the form of criticism. Token appreciation could be found with teachers and sports coaches, but even that form of encouragement was usually associated with a dose of criticism and the advice to do better next time. I guess, for me, I had to adapt to obtaining adult attention through criticism; at least then I knew I was alive.

Wes – 63

Acknowledging is about seeing what's wonderful and amazing in a young man, lifting his self-esteem, and letting him know he has value in your eyes. Unless boys threaten you and yours, let someone else play the cop or disciplinarian. Just go with acknowledgement. You'll know you're on the right track when you see the boy's reaction. Most often there will be a shy but almost immediate and positive response. Because it's such an uncommon experience in their lives, you may even notice a little shock or surprise. What will very quickly become obvious is that you have, in a small way, in that moment, made a positive difference in a young man's life.

Blessing Boys

I call the next step *Blessing* because there is something a little spiritual about clearly noticing and then telling someone how they are unique and wonderful. Blessing a young male is a very powerful statement about him, your connection to him, and his place in the masculine order of things. A blessing goes beyond the positive comment in passing we discussed as an acknowledgement. It's an intimate and positive statement about a young man's value, potential, person, or power . . . and it's designed to touch the receiver at his core.

On my graduation day, my school superintendent totally surprised me when he congratulated me. He said,

"Dustin, I hope we get more kids like you at our school. You are going to do great in life." It was extremely uplifting and I will remember his comment for the rest of my life.

Dustin – 20

Blessing happens when an adult male catches a young guy doing something especially well or identifies one of his positive attributes, skills, or tendencies. The man then names what he sees and adds a statement of value. In the process, the boy is not only acknowledged, but is further elevated to a place of heightened esteem. If you actually know the young man, your observation will have the weight of your history together hanging on it. The better you know the young man, the more you *get* him, the more potent your blessing will be.

I recall one time when I was in the prison system when one of the staff read a short essay I had written. I don't remember what it was about but he complimented me saying my essay was "analytical and introspective." I took in these positive strokes and from then on identified myself as a "good writer." This encouraged me to write later on in life.

Dwayne – 25

One of the reasons blessings are so powerful is they're uncommon. So seldom are blessings offered to young males, some of us, many years later, can remember special blessings we received from men in the past. For the same reason, it's very possible your blessing of a boy will be his first or will become the powerful memory that will stay with him a lifetime. Blessings provide so much transformational energy for such little effort, it's amazing they're not a bigger part of all our lives.

I know from my own life that just a few words can have an incredible impact on a young man's life. I still remember something one of my favorite teachers said to me. "Cris, you're very creative. Keep writing. You never know who is reading your story." He saw past my bad spelling and my anger and saw my talent and desire to communicate, to tell my story. Those fourteen words had a huge and lasting impact.

Cris – 53

If being blessed was not a part of your boyhood, you may not have a model for affirming a boy in this way. In that case, the skill of blessing a young man can take some effort to learn and practice until it's comfortable. First, you have to believe your blessing is wanted, needed, and will have positive impact. The second step is to be on the lookout for the strengths, talents, and character in the young men around you. Then all that remains is to find the courage to actually step forward and tell a young man what you see. Once you've tried it a few times, the boy's reaction will provide all the reinforcement you need to continue.

For me, young guys I see on bikes, blades, or skateboards, showing off their usually considerable athletic talents, are good candidates for a blessing. In those moments I try to say something like, "Ya know, dude, I've seen a lot of guys in this skateboard park doing amazing things, but that last rail you did was really awesome. That took incredible balance, strength, and a bagful of courage. Very nice ride, man."

Without too much difficulty, I can always find something unique, amazing, or curious about a young man. From experience, I've learned it takes very little effort to take the next step of saying something to him that has a positive spin. I've learned from their reactions it's simply a good thing to do, and I really enjoy the feeling I get as a result.

I'm very sad to say, I cannot remember one positive comment from a man in my youth. I remember quite a few incidents in which my father or a football coach told me what a loser I was, but never a positive. I'm now fully recovered. Several decades back, I felt I had finally proven myself a fit human being and satisfied my long-dead father. If you wanted positives as told to me by a woman, I could name many.

Earl W. – 74

You may have had the good fortune to have experienced the occasional elder blessing and have some personal sense of its power. If you haven't been blessed in recent history, let me help right now by giving *you* a blessing.

I recognize you are the kind of man who cares enough about boys to take the time and energy to read this book. I honor you for your open heart, your ability to see boys need your support, and for simply considering how you might get more involved. Because of who you are, I know you must be already making a difference somewhere. I'm excited about the additional gifts you'll bring to the young guys around you when you step into action. From one man to another, thank you for being you. I am very proud of you.

How did that feel? It's true I don't know you personally, but because you're reading this book, I feel I can honestly make that statement. You can imagine how the potency of a blessing can increase with the quality of the connection and a little history between the younger male and the man offering the blessing. Whenever a blessing is true and it's offered with sincerity, it will hit the mark with profoundly positive impact.

Not only are you changed by seeing the impact of your comments on the young man, you are hearing the blessing and also being changed. When you bless a young guy, you improve the masculine esteem of two males and are firmly engaged in the business of man-making.

> I was a violent, angry young man. There was no one, I mean no one that I would not or did not threaten to kill if they pissed me off. But then I got a series of huge blessings when three guys, Waid M., Guy A., and my track coach all came into my life at the same time. Like the Perfect Storm, there was enough energy among these three men to calm the riot going on inside of me. They all saw my potential and were strong enough to tell me that I was "better than that" when I started to escalate. Because of them, I went from failing to honor role in a very short time. I know those guys were proud of me, and proud of themselves for saving a tough kid. It was a gift from them that I can only repay today by seeking out and serving men and boys in return.
>
> Jon – 54

In making these suggestions, I'm not talking about seeing, acknowledging, and blessing only the boys you may know. I'm talking about stepping up for the large group of young males I call OPBs, or Other People's Boys. ANY boy you encounter during your day should be seen as an opportunity for this form of man-making. Once you resolve to acknowledge boys in this way, you will find opportunities abound. Rest assured, whether young males look like it or not, every boy you come across is starving for your attention and positive acknowledgement. Because of this hunger, you simply can't make a mistake or do it wrong.

As you'll soon be learning, guiding a young man toward a positive manhood requires many different kinds of inputs from many different men. Up to this point, we've been discussing the informal approaches: Just Being You, and Seeing, Acknowledging, and Blessing young males you encounter as you move through your daily life. For the most part, these actions are intentional but random events, and they require the least commitment. As long as there have been men and boys, these actions have been important and necessary ways of guiding boys on their journey to manhood . . . important and necessary, but not enough. In the next chapter, we'll explore other man-making actions that require a little more of your time and commitment to boys . . . positive actions that will have an even greater impact on you and the young males involved.

4

One-to-Many Man-Making

When men are a regular part of a boy's life, the young man gets to see manhood modeled over time. These connections give a boy the opportunity to learn what men do, how they think, what they attend to, how they relate to others, and how men process feelings. With men to learn from, a boy might pick up some of the skills or interests the men share. In so many ways and without much effort, a man is actively training a younger male for manhood by simply being a consistent presence in his life.

After the actions of seeing, acknowledging, and blessing boys, the next level of involvement includes activities where there is one, or a group men, with many boys. In the two sections of this chapter, you'll find many examples of these kinds of activities. You'll also learn about men, just like you, who have found meaningful ways to make a difference in the lives of many boys. The first section is titled, Create-Your-Own Man-Making, and it's about how you can share your hobbies or personal interests with a group of boys. The second section is titled, Volunteer Man-Making, and it describes some of the many ways men can volunteer to be involved with groups of boys. If the one-man-to-many-boys form of man-making appeals to you, there is a good chance you'll find an activity that will call you into action in the examples that follow.

Create-Your-Own Man-Making

One very successful approach to being a one-to-many man-maker is to simply take what you love doing and figure out how to do it in a way that can involve boys. If you have a hobby such as fishing, computers, carpentry, stamps, roller blading, boxing, working at the humane society, playing music, chess… or anything you're interested in, you have something to offer a group of boys. For man-making to happen, however, you do have to be willing to share your interest with the people around you. It's best to start with the boys and men you already know. First, ask them if they have any interest in learning about your hobby. If other men's experience is any predictor, once you have a few interested males, it will be easy to expand your circle. You can also generate interest by:

- simply letting people in your neighborhood know about your interest and that you'd like to spend time with others pursuing the activity;

- holding a session on the topic at your place of worship, or offering to teach a class at a school;

- putting an ad in the community paper describing your interest or, even better, having someone from the paper interview you;

- using my favorite approach, some evening invite a few men and boys you all know over to learn about your hobby.

If you find a way to let the world know what you have to offer, boys and other men will find you, and some serious man-making will commence. Here are just a few examples of what I and other men have done to connect with boys and men in our communities.

Hiking

In the winter, my wife and I live in Tucson, Arizona, near the foothills of the Catalina Mountains. I love heading off in the mornings to hike when the birds are singing and the musty smell of the dew on the desert is still in the air. I had been hanging out with a teenage guy named Kevin, and I suggested he join me on my morning hike some time. After a number of invites, he took me up on my offer and we finally hit the trail. I did have to compromise with him in that, like most guys his age, he was so NOT a morning person.

I had mentioned this hike to some of my men friends, and they asked if we do it again, they'd like to bring some of the young males they knew. The following year, I put out the call and a larger group of men and boys hit the trail. The hike is now an annual boys' and men's tradition. Sharing my passion for hiking was just that simple.

> What I liked about the hike was that it was fun, it was outdoors, I didn't have to worry about "normal" life, and the older guys respected us and didn't treat us like lessers.
>
> Jack – 12

Since the first group outing, a template for a perfect boys' hike has evolved. The hikes now always include some boy-sized vertical climbs for a sense of achievement. There are pre-hike warnings about what to do if we encounter a snake or mountain lion (small chance, but adds a sense of adventure). There is always at least one big vista point (for the "mom photo"), and the hike is just long enough to make the boys, and many of the men, feel as if they have gone on an adventure and earned some bragging rights. On a typical hike, there are 15-20 males who range in age from nine to mid-sixties. I just love seeing men and boys in single file on a trail. I know this is what males have done for centuries, it feels very right to everyone, and it makes me very happy. With any luck, the tradition will continue far into the future.

Woodworking

I can remember being in the seventh grade and going to my first woodworking class at Randolph Heights Elementary School in St. Paul, Minnesota. I clearly remember walking into the shop room and immediately being in awe of the husky wooden workbenches, the heavy vises, all the tools hanging in place on the walls, and especially the smell of freshly sawed lumber. The man who commanded the place, Mr. Wilson, was big, hairy, and had a way of looking hard at us that said, "don't even think about screwing up." When Mr. Wilson laid out the plans for the footstool that was to become our project, I wondered how we were ever going to turn all those pictures and lines into a real object. More than fifty years later, I still have that little stool in my closet and a happy memory of his class.

I teach woodworking classes for young boys and men. I am very deliberate in my speech and behavior with them. It always starts out the same way. "Tell me about yourself, what you want to learn, and what you already know." Then on to my commitment, "My prime directive is safety. I will do everything I can to keep you safe." In my classes, I have four rules. Rule 1: Safety, Safety, and Safety. Rule 2: If you do not understand, ask. Rule 3: I am not your parent; clean up after yourself. Rule 4: Have fun. With all that agreed upon, we move on to creating amazing things out of wood.

Cris – 53

Men who enjoy making things out of wood can sometimes help in a woodworking class at a school or for a scout troop. If you have the interest and some tools, you can simply get some boys together and build something in your garage. There must be an ancient imprint in the male brain for guys getting together using tools because it feels so natural and right. Even making something as simple as a stool is sure to capture the attention and imagination of a young guy. The activity will allow countless opportunities to teach and compliment your understudies on their growing skills. It will also quickly elevate you to the status of esteemed expert in their eyes.

When I was in Cub Scouts at around ten years old, for two years my den master was a guy named Mr. Albert. He was an awesome guy. He wouldn't let us kids get out of hand, and he did weird things like make waffles for supper! He was really good with tools and did lots of remodeling around his house. He rebuilt his whole kitchen himself in his spare time. One cool thing Mr. Albert did was make sure we entered the Pinwood Derby. He helped each of us build a little racing car in his woodshop out in his garage.

I was really sad when he stopped doing Scouts. I don't even know where my dad is, and my mom never married anyone else, and now there's not really anyone who's a male role model for me. I guess that's OK because I want to be like Mr. Albert anyway. He's a hard worker, a nice guy, and I don't remember ever seeing him lose his temper. And I want a workshop like his someday too.

Nat – 15

Brad Buxton is a man with a passion for woodworking and for building boats. I discovered him in an article in my local newspaper, describing his work with kids. Brad has done carpentry and cabinetry and built boats for years. As an outgrowth of his interest, he found himself teaching boat-building to a class of fifth graders at The Science Museum of Minnesota. Brad liked that experience so much he decided to focus his energy on young people.

With a little help from interested and supportive adults, in 1995, Brad formed Urban Boatbuilders, Inc., or UBI (urbanboatbuilders.org) as a non-profit organization. Since then, by working with different schools, churches, and after-school programs, hundreds of young people have taken part in UBI's many boat-building and related activities. UBI's mission is "To share knowledge and provide opportunities for youth to develop positive skills, attitudes, and connections to their communities and to local water resources through the building and use of boats."

At the UBI workshop in St. Paul, young people find a safe, friendly, and very cooperative environment. They build competition boats, river skiffs, and rowboats. Through the cultural boatbuilding program, kids study other cultures and then build culturally relevant boats. In the process, they also find important connections to adults who have an interest in helping young people.

One powerful example of UBI's ability to touch boys' lives has been the Wednesday Evening Program. On Wednesday evenings, boys who are in the juvenile justice system and sentenced to a residential facility, are brought to the UBI workshop to learn about boat-building and have some positive interaction with the UBI men. Through UBI's work with more than fifteen different local organizations since 1996, three hundred kids a year will get the benefit of Brad's commitment, experience, and passion. Brad is one serious man-maker and an incredible community resource. His enormous impact on the males in his community all started with his love of woodworking and a willingness to share his passion.

Reading

I was not having much luck trying to get Barry, a thirteen-year-old friend of mine, to keep his brain alive over his summer vacation by reading. Barry enjoys being constantly active, and as a teenager, he always had better things to do than read in the summer. When I shared my challenge of getting him interested in books, a friend told me about Guys Read, a web-based literacy program for boys. It's an initiative that was born out of Jon Scieszka's passion to get boys to read. You can learn all about it at guysread.com. Jon taught elementary school for ten years, raised a daughter and son, and has written a number of books for kids. Jon notes, "A lot of boys are having trouble reading," and lists the following data as testimony:

- The U.S. Department of Education reading tests for the last thirty years show boys scoring worse than girls do in every age group, every year.

- Eighth-grade boys are 50% more likely than girls to be held back a year.

- Two-thirds of Special Education students in high school are boys.

- Overall college enrollment is higher for girls than for boys.

For these reasons, part of Jon's mission is to "…motivate boys to read by connecting them with materials they will want to read." Given the computer literacy of today's young males, Jon's website is a great way to accomplish that goal. His site is extremely boy-oriented, fun, and very usable. The site provides a list of recommended books, as well as a search engine that allows searches by a favorite book, favorite author, or simply a subject or topic. If you know a young guy who could use some motivation to read, point him at this site and see what happens. Because of

Guys Read, my pal Barry now has a short reading list that he's actually excited about.

Jon says it's time to "make some noise for boys." He points out, "We have literacy programs for adults and families, and Guys Read is our chance to call attention to boys' literacy."

Out of Jon's teaching experience and his concern for boys, he's developed an extremely creative approach to a huge problem. Jon is another great role model for any man who has experience with a hobby or interest and is considering reaching out to boys. What would the world be like if every adult man, like Jon, reached into his deep reservoir of knowledge, experience, and interests and turned them into something to help boys?

Sports

Men teaching boys about any activity that involves competition and objects flying through space is an ancient practice and a sure-fire, one-to-many approach to man-making. We're not talking about coaching a sports team yet... that will come later. This man-making activity is simply about taking a sport you enjoy and then finding a way to fold in the boys. Golf, archery, bowling, Frisbee golf, orienteering, mountain biking... any sport you enjoy can quickly become interesting to a group of young guys.

A man who is in a men's organization with me, thirty-eight-year-old Patrick, discovered the man-making potential in the Olympic sport of curling. Curling is similar to shuffleboard. It is played by teams, indoors, and on a sheet of ice 142 feet long. Here is how Patrick describes his experience.

> When I learned to curl, I had a very patient teacher by the name of Seppo. At sixteen years my senior, Seppo was a gentleman, role model, and the perfect older male guide. He took the time to teach me about the sport, train me in delivery and sweeping techniques, and all about the his-

tory and etiquette of the game. Because of Seppo's influence, later in my life I again took up the sport of curling with my children at the local curling center. It wasn't long after that I found myself involved teaching a group of nine boys.

The group of boys I initially worked with has grown and I now oversee the entire junior program. This year we have seventy-eight students ranging in age from eight to twenty-one years of age. I spend my time with them working on various skills, and teaching them to be fine young men on and off the ice. The group of boys I work most closely with are the ones where I see something in them that reminds me of myself when I was that age. These are the boys where it's clear they need a man from outside their family to affirm them as young men.

I believe teaching boys about a sport is a great way to develop positive character traits that will help them throughout their lives. When we're on the ice, we talk about how to be a good winner or loser, how to treat our opponents, how to treat teammates, how to behave when the outcome of a game is on the line, and how your attitude can be affected by others.

Patrick says another time where a lot of training takes place is when the team is travelling. Away from parents, the kids tend to become loud and occasionally obnoxious. He says, "As a respected older man, this gives me a chance to shape their behavior in some important ways while letting them know I care about them. I find many opportunities to teach these guys some basic social skills, such as etiquette at the table; about politeness (not burping out loud); how, when, and why to tip a server; and other simple but important talents. I am the first to be playful, but they know there are rules to be followed. Overall, it's a truly awesome experience."

Any sport, because of its physicality, learning opportunities, and competition in a tribe of boys and men, is a perfect man-making environment for young males. If you have a love for a particular sport, any sport, consider inviting some boys along on your next outing.

Driving

Jay Gubrud is a friend of mine and is a man who loves driving BMW automobiles ... fast. He is a member of the BMW Car Club of Minnesota, a group that has a focus on safe and skillful driving. Through the club, Jay learned that the National Highway Traffic Administration statistics say motor vehicle crashes are the leading cause of death among teenagers in the United States. In addition, the U.S. Center for Disease Control and Prevention reports crash risk for drivers sixteen and seventeen years old is three times as great as it is for nineteen and twenty-year-olds. In every age category, the crash and death statistics are worse for boys than girls. Those numbers got Jay's attention and he decided to do something.

Like most teens, Jay had developed an early love of driving fast. He said he wished he'd had a high-performance driving program available to him in adolescence, when his love of driving was blooming. In Jay's words, "My dad had no interest in driving or performance driving so I had to learn from the school of hard knocks. If there would have been someone steering me toward safe driving at that point in my life, I'd have had a lot fewer problems." Jay said, just like he did, most teens find out the limitations of their skills on public roads, surrounded by other vehicles, in dangerous, real-world conditions, and often with the police involved. He saw a big need to help teenagers become more skillful drivers.

As a direct result of his passion, Jay partnered with the BMW Club of Minnesota to create the Safe Teen Driving Program. The program initially put fourteen Minneapolis and St. Paul area teens in the capable hands of instructors from the BMW Club. These people led the students through classroom and on-road training. Instead of taking risks on the street, the kids are able to develop their skills and discover the limits of their vehicles on a safe and custom-made track. Since that first event, hundreds of Minnesota teens have successfully completed this program. While all teens, regardless of gender, need to learn how to become the best possible drivers, young male drivers, with their tendencies for testing their limits and risk-taking in general, stand to gain the most from this kind of training.

Because of his passion for driving, Jay not only helped to create a solid safe driving program for kids, in the process he may have prevented serious injury or death for a teenage boy or girl. His story gets even better, however. The BMW Car Club of America used much of the Safe Teen Driving Program in the development of a national program now called *Street Survival* (streetsurvival.org). Acting on his interest in driving, Jay has touched the lives of many thousands of kids all across the U.S.A.

Computers

Computers today make up a wonderful and mysterious universe, full of endless challenges and learning opportunities. I'll admit I just love tinkering with both the hardware and software. The general rule in computing is if you're six months farther along on the learning curve than the person you're helping, you're a genius.

Based on that premise, I volunteered at a vocational high school in Tucson, Arizona, and became their unofficial Webmaster. I worked with a half-dozen kids, mostly guys, who were interested in computers and the Internet. With a little combined effort, we created a website for the school. It was a funky, teen-relevant, and thanks to me, technologically imperfect site. Nevertheless, it was visible to the whole world and the kids were proud of the parts they created and published. The school's management was happy because the kids were learning important skills and the site was a great marketing tool for the high school.

I enjoyed sharing my knowledge, finding ways to celebrate each of the kids, and the general process of learning our way through problems together. Because it was mostly a male group, it was also a great man-making activity. The school has grown and gone on to a fancier website now. I think a lot has been lost by not having a kid-built site and a supportive volunteer working with them. For the record, I had zero training for a teaching role. Yet, I find my empathy for the kids, my interest in computers, and a little creativity somehow made it all work.

Guy Time

A group of my men friends enjoy the occasional game of paintball. Paintball is a sport where you dress in protective gear, carry a compressed air gun that shoots a marble-sized ball filled with colored liquid, and then chase each other around in the woods. I suggested we add some young guys to our outing for more challenge, and to see if we couldn't teach them some things about guns, stalking, and even war. Each of us gathered up a young guy or two we knew and headed for the paintball range.

After arrival at the range, but prior to heading out into the fields, we had a serious discussion about guns, shooting people, and the feelings of anger and a desire for revenge. A couple of the men who were combat veterans spoke to the guys about the ugly realities of being in a war. It was good to hear the men and boys sharing their complicated thoughts and feelings on these hard topics. By the end of the discussion, we were clear our day was going to be about having fun, playing together, and enjoying the day.

We learned all the rules of the field that would keep it a safe activity for everyone, and even invented a few of our own guidelines. For example, we decided to change team members after each of the seven rounds so it wouldn't get too competitive and to avoid feelings of anger and the desire for revenge we had learned about earlier. With our agreements in place, we started and quickly got in touch with our male instincts for being in the woods and stalking each other. It was fun, physical, ever so slightly "dangerous," and very much "guy time."

As we've been discussing, a boy learns how to be a man in large part by watching and listening to men. For that reason alone, any activity a boy shares with you and other men is good for him. In fact, the more men who are involved, the more "male" the activity, and the more valuable the experience will be for him.

"Guy time" might be paying a young man to be a caddy when you go golfing with your men friends. It could be inviting some young guys to join your men friends working on a construction project, or taking them camping. Any activity that involves being around a group of men is inherently satisfying for an adolescent male, and you'll be starting or deepening what could become a long-term connection. On these "guy" activities, the boy or boys you invite will hear men tell stories, listen to men talk about women, pass gas (bonding), learn older guy humor, and they will struggle mightily to look good in the company of their male elders.

The unconscious desire to enter the men's hut, wherever it's found, is hardwired into adolescent males. Young males want and need access to that male place, unconstrained by feminine influence, where male forms of relating and processing dominate. It's where *male* stories, experiences, humor, pain, comforting, compassion, and truth are shared. It's where the essence of masculinity resides, and the place where an adolescent male will get the perfect form of nourishment required for his journey to manhood to be successful.

When you include a young man in activities that involve other men, you're letting him peek inside that sacred male place, allowing him to *absorb* manhood, and strengthening your connection to him.

• • • • •

The men profiled in these Create-Your-Own Man-Making examples are men just like you. They didn't have any special training, they were simply willing to risk sharing their gifts and interests with others. Don't underestimate the power to change boys' lives by simply sharing your interest or hobby. The only real barriers are those negative messages in your head saying, "I really don't have anything to offer," "it will never work," "I'll mess up somehow," …or a million other lies. If you can rise above all that chatter, you'll hear the boys calling for your presence and influence in their lives. THAT is the important message to hear.

Volunteer Man-Making

There are many ways to get involved with one-to-many man-making when you volunteer with a group already at work in your community providing activities for young males. These groups often come with ready-made community approval and time-tested approaches for their activities. With some groups, you'll get some training, but mostly, you'll just have to step up and learn from experience. However, in most volunteer man-making, you'll have the added benefit of drawing upon the encouragement and experience of many other involved adults. Because of all these supports, this type of man-making can be a great place to begin your man-making with a group of boys.

You make me want to be a better man!
  – Jack Nicholson as Melvin Udall,
        from the film *As Good as It Gets*

Because of the enormous need for adult male volunteers, it will take very little effort for you to find a welcoming group. For your inspiration, what follows are descriptions of just a few of the many readily available opportunities for one-to-many man-making found in most communities.

Coaching

Any kind of male team activity or sport is a natural and organic form of man-making. Being on a team also gives young guys a chance to belong to something that's positive and adult male supported. Being a coach, by definition, means you literally have the power to shape young male lives in a thousand positive ways.

You don't even have to have experience with the particular sport to be of enormous value. School teams, Little League teams, parks and recreation programs, community-based soccer, hockey, or baseball leagues, and many other groups in every community need men to volunteer. If you don't want full coaching responsibilities, it won't be hard to find a head coach who needs other men to assist. Men are needed to supervise parts of a practice, go along on road games, and provide the masculine authority necessary to contain all the young male energy on a sports team.

Bob L. was my first coach in baseball and his son, Danny, was my best friend. Danny played second base, but Bob moved him to shortstop so I could play second (my arm was not strong enough at that time to play shortstop). He gave me the opportunity to play the sport I loved at a position where I could excel. A couple of years later, as my arm grew strong, in addition to playing second base, he let me pitch. I became an all-star at both positions. When I moved to another town just before my sophomore year in high school, Bob told the coach at the new school about me. That gave me a head start in being welcomed in the new community. Bob was always the coach and he always built me up. He increased my confidence and helped me achieve new heights. I owe him a lot.

                                                                Mark – 33

Coaching is hard work that often takes place at inconvenient times. Getting the attention of a pack of adolescent males, much less keeping it focused while developing their athletic and team skills, is very challenging work. However, the rewards from this high order of man-making are enormous for both the coaches and the boys. A man named Doug, now sixty-five, describes his first baseball coach with a deep reverence.

My first baseball coach, Merrel, was a former minor league star, crippled in an automobile accident. He and his wife ran a small confectionery for their livelihood and it was the hangout for those he coached and many others. I found out just after my ninth birthday that Merrel wanted me to tryout for the baseball team, and from that day on, he was one of my strongest supporters.

Merrel taught me everything about the game of baseball, including how to win and lose comfortably. I can still visualize him balanced on his crutches while hitting infield practice. His courage, friendship, acceptance, and humor were hallmarks of this remarkable human. After we grew too old to play on his teams, my pals and I continued to visit Rook's Confectionery, even when we came home from college.

Merrel was the first visitor at my father's wake and our hug was wonderfully sustaining. Not too many months after my father's death, I heard that Merrel had died of a heart attack. His large funeral, in addition to people my age, was heavily populated by lots of young people who also treasured his gifts of support and friendship.

There is little question about the enormous positive influence a good coach has in boys' lives. For many men, the impact of having a solid, caring, and no-nonsense man in charge of growing them into athletes is an important part of their life story. Joshua, a young man of twenty-two, describes his volunteer experience as a high school hockey coach.

> During practices, I would encourage the boys and push them to do their best. I tried to get them to understand they may not be able to control certain circumstances, and they can't control the way others act. What they can control are their own actions, and most importantly, their attitude. I found that by simply believing in a boy, having faith that he will succeed at what he whole-heartedly strives for, encourages him to have faith in himself. Being on a disciplined team gives boys a place and a purpose. When boys feel there is a purpose for them, and that someone believes in them, they feel whole, worthy, and special. Actually, being a coach made me a better man too.

When you find a place to volunteer, I guarantee the impact on you will also be life-changing. A very dear friend of mine, Bob R., died a few years back. On one visit just a week before his death, Bob told me a story about his hockey coaching days that touched both of us.

> I was attending a community gathering in my honor. In the social time after the speeches, a forty-one-year-old man approached me. The guy asked me, "Are you Mr. R?" I said yes, I am. Then he introduced himself as one of "your hockey players." He said I was the best damn coach he

ever had and that he had to come to thank me for everything. The man said, "You taught us how to lose as well as
win and gave our team a heart." I thanked him and asked
him how he recognized me after thirty-one years. He said,
"I recognized your smile."

It was a beautiful story that had stayed with Bob for years and
seemed to have special importance with Bob's death in the wings.
The tears we were crying together at his telling of that story were
testimony to the legacy and impact of coaching on both men and
boys.

Scouting

One organization in which boys have been very successfully mentored by men is scouting. In America, scouting has been around
more than a hundred years and has more than 300 local coun-
cils. Scouting serves both boys and girls from the ages of seven
to twenty regardless of their race, creed, economic, or social status. The core program, Boy Scouts, is open to boys, ages eleven
through seventeen, and is a proven and successful approach to
man-making.

Scouting is a volunteer movement that uses both adult and
youth leaders. In doing so, it builds relationships between boys
and older males of differing ages. Given its history and highly
structured programs, scouting provides an easy path for men to
step into this approach to man-making.

Cub Scouts and Boy Scouts gave me a whole community of male role models. We got together regularly for
meetings. I remember preparing as a team for a jubilee,
and learning how to tie knots in a rope that was as thick
as your fist. We learned first aid and earned merit badges
by demonstrating the skills we learned within our troop.
In Cub Scouts, you walked over the bridge of light to

receive your arrow of light and drink the buffalo's blood,
which turned out to be V8 tomato juice. I remember
memorizing the Boy Scout motto, and other words like
truth, responsibility, loyalty, honesty, bravery, and courage,
describing what it meant to be a man of honor. Each step
from Cub Scout to Boy Scout, and then to Eagle Scout,
represented the next change in my life from boyhood to
manhood. I loved it.

Bill – 25

The goals of scouting are to build personal and team skills,
reward accomplishment in a wide variety of content areas, and,
as a result, to create young people of good moral character. While
local activities can vary greatly, scouting offers many of the kinds
of activities that are perfect for a young man's development and
just happen to be a good environment for adult male volunteers.
Just a few of the character-shaping experiences a guy will find in
scouting include:

A positive hierarchy. Because males always want to know
their place in the order of things, the structured levels of advancement and status they earn in scouting, all the way up to Eagle
Scout, are compelling. The rank of Eagle is at the top and it's a
lifetime achievement award earned by only 2% of all Boy Scouts.
Boys who have come up through this ladder of challenges always
report they had life- and character-shaping experiences.

When faced with new challenges in my life today, I
often reach into that well of leadership, self-confidence,
and ingenuity taught to me in my advancement through
Scouting. I am still proud to be an Eagle Scout.

Dean H. – 51

When there are enough men involved, a boy will have plenty
of adult males, elders, and heroes to emulate. As a boy progresses

through the different stages of Scouting, he will also have a chance to demonstrate leadership and see himself as a guide for the younger males.

Opportunities for learning, advancement, recognition, and reward. Moving from Tenderfoot through Eagle Scout is a path designed to build a boy's self-esteem, self-confidence, and life skills through a progressive set of challenges, surmountable obstacles, and support to work toward achievable goals. One example is the diverse merit badge program, which allows each boy to create his own, self-paced educational path, based on personal interests. This process creates many opportunities for a boy to sample a variety of potential subjects, have a sense of achievement, and get positive recognition from adults and his peers.

A chance to be outdoors. Many Scout troops provide the opportunity for young guys to spend time in the great outdoors, being vigorously active, exploring, learning, and playing games. It also creates the perfect natural environment for leaders to use rituals, fire, "trials," and storytelling, all of which are age-old components of the man-making experience.

If this kind of organization appeals to you, scouting offers countless opportunities for you to rediscover parts of your boyhood you may have missed. You will also find esteem-building activities, an enormous sense of accomplishment, connection to more experienced men, and most importantly, the ability to see the young people in your charge benefit from your involvement.

Volunteering at Your Place of Worship

Volunteering at your place of worship to teach, work, or support others in activities are all good ways of having a positive impact on the young males in your faith community. Today, many places of worship have special youth programs for their kids and even reach out to the kids in the surrounding community. These groups can use your help.

> Unlike a lot of people I know, I have pretty much always had a really good relationship with my dad. However, by the time I was sixteen my parents had broken up and I had lost a lot of respect for any adults. I had been disillusioned by the divorce, high school life, and people overall. I never went over the edge, but I did start drinking and using drugs.
>
> Eventually, a Christian friend brought me to church one day, where I met an associate pastor who accepted me in spite of all my youthful baggage. Now, five years later, we are still great friends. He performed my marriage ceremony and was one of the first people I called when my two sons were born. We are planning to be around each other for a long time to come.
>
> Nathan – 22

Michael O. is sixty and an amazing man-maker in his spiritual community. He decided to help form and run a group for guys at his church. This is what Michael said: "I'm part of a church-based group for young men called the TAG group. It stands for Totally Awesome Guys, and it's been a great experience for me. The men in the group are the minister, the youth leader, myself, and another retired man. There are eight boys who have volunteered to be in the group, and they range in age from thirteen to sixteen years old. We meet weekly at the church during the school year.

In our meetings, we begin with a shared meal and then have a brief prayer before we open up the group for any topic the boys bring up. The subjects range from the trivial to very serious topics such as death, struggles with relationships, friends in trouble, divorce... all things that are common issues for adolescent boys today. I believe these rather deep exchanges can take place because of the rules we have around confidentiality, respectful listening, and the fact that the men also share from their own lives. With the obvious commitment of the men, the boys feel safe, cared about, and that it's OK to be open. With each closing circle and prayer, we feel a little closer and trust each other more. It feels good to be a role model and it's been amazing to experience the boys' capacity for intimate discussion."

Should you decide to volunteer at your place of worship, just your visible presence in your spiritual community would be a statement that spirituality is an important element of manhood. In the same way boys are curious about how men think, feel, and what they do for work, they also want to know what you believe in and why. If you are prepared to stand up for your spiritual values and your involvement allows for dialogue with boys, you will have plenty of chances to use your man-making influence to help shape the spiritual beliefs of young men.

Camp Counseling

I can remember going to a week-long, summer *YMCA* camp for boys when I was about ten. Looking back, I realize it must have been barely controlled chaos for the staff, but for me it was a wild-eyed adventure. I can remember the bunkhouse beds, the smell of the wooden camp buildings, running around in tribes with Native American names, learning how to paddle a canoe, and how to carve wood with a buck knife. As we sat around the fires at night, there were marshmallows to roast, songs to sing, and scary stories the counselors told. Of course, it was there I went on my first snipe hunt. Through it all, there were always older men and boys who became my heroes. Returning home with my new knowledge, experiences, and friends, I always felt I was a little more of a man than the boy who'd left. Going off to camp with men and boys, with all of its adventure and magical elements, was just the right mix of ingredients at that time in my life.

Many of the men who contributed to my man-making research reported positive memories about the discovery, the counselors, and new friends they made when they went away to a camp. Here are just a few of the many stories men shared.

> I was a counselor staffing a young men's adventure weekend near Vancouver, British Columbia. The weekend provided young men with individual and team challenges, and lots of adult males around. There was an older boy, about seventeen, attempting to control others with his hot temper. I and three other men sat him down and really listened to him. He really wasn't having fun and wanted to leave. It may have been the first time in his life he felt he was really heard. We gave him a clear choice and he decided to stay. By the time the camp ended, he had started to shift his behavior.
>
> Six months later, I was giving two women friends a ride to the airport and they were talking about one of their sons. I recognized the boy they were talking about as the young man from camp. His mother said until he went to the weekend, he had a lot of depression, was hurting him-self, and considering suicide. Since his camp experience, he has shifted his outlook on his life and become much more positive. This experience taught me that you may never know the impact you can have on a boy by investing just a little of your time and attention.
>
> Cole – 54

> I was a counselor at a church camp for three weeks during my eleventh and twelfth grades. I had six camp-ers in my unit who were seventh- and eighth-grade boys. Part of my role was to keep them in line, yet give them enough freedom to have fun. Church camp is the place where many kids have their first dating experience. Many

of the girls actually were the more aggressive in making the "date," mostly to just hold hands and walk off into the woods. In some cases, kids actually have their first kiss at church camp. It is a safe place, after all.

One night, when the boys were refusing to go to sleep, I took it on myself to teach them what kissing was all about. As my campers lay speechless in their bunks, in a very soft voice I described your average kissing, ear kissing, and even French kissing. The latter drew predictable groans, but they listened intently to every word I was saying. I knew at some level church camp was not the place to talk about sex, but it actually turned out to be the best place. Being in an all-male cabin, with the lights off, and an older male instructing them in what life is all about, was perfect.

After sharing this secret information, I left the cabin in total silence as the boys pretended to be asleep. But I hung out by the back window to hear their reaction after I left. It was fun and interesting to hear how they, each in his own way, tried to assimilate this new and important information from an adult.

Mark – 58

Many organizations offer camping experiences. The focus of the camp might be computers, sports training, nature study, language, music, skateboarding, learning to jump on a trampoline, or any of a multitude of other possibilities. What they all have in common is they need men to get involved. If this kind of experience sounds interesting to you, find a camp that matches your interests and volunteer to help. The rewards will be enormous.

I worked as a camp counselor for three summers at a camp in northeastern Minnesota. Since I had attended camp as a youngster and enjoyed it, I decided to go and give something back. What I found is the youngsters really look up to you. Everything you do is, in a way, sucked into their heads. They want to be "cool" like their counselor. I particularly enjoyed leading songs at campfire. It was really a magical type of experience for the boys and for me.

Justin – 29

Volunteering at School

Volunteering at a school is an important way to be involved with man-making. Most schools need and want more men to balance out a primarily female teaching staff. Whether volunteering at a school to help with reading classes, building things in after-school programs, helping teach a foreign language, or talking to a class about your profession, a man showing up in school is a gift to everyone, but especially the boys.

One of the ways I am getting involved in boys' lives is that next month I will be addressing about thirty twelve-year-old boys at their school about the benefits of reading. As you may be aware, Australia has huge literacy problems with boys. So, my aim is to simply tell boys what I was reading at that age, what type of books inspired me to continue reading, and what sort of material I'm reading these days.

David – 47

When I spoke with forty-four-year-old Christopher, he told me a story that expressed the specific kind of impact a caring adult male can have on boys in a school setting.

My kids' school took fifth-grade kids away for a few days each year to a nature camp where they had a guided walk and group activities. They made it work by getting parents to volunteer as chaperones. These boys were naturally bouncing off the walls for much of the trip. I remember being firm but fair and getting them organized, ready, and behaving appropriately through much of the camp.

Of the boys that I chaperoned, one was "that kid"— you know him because every school has him. He was a bully, loud, ADD, and uncontrolled, giving lip to everyone and being disrespectful of adults. The woman who organized the trip actually apologized in advance when she included him in my little pack, but eventually, even he fell in line.

Years later, my son shared with me why he thought the boys in my group toed the line so well. He reminded me that I have a speech habit with younger boys that I take for granted. I allowed them to call me "Chris" and I referred to them by their first names when they were behaving. When they were misbehaving, I referred to them as Mr. McDowel, Mr. Crosby, or Mr. Smith in a stern tone to let them know they were on the edge of trouble with me. When I spoke to them in a group setting or in front of the other adults, I referred to them as gentlemen rather than boys. My son told me years later, he and the other boys always liked being treated like young men rather than little kids.

Pick a school, introduce yourself, and maybe even suggest a project you would like to do. Take this book along and tell them you have been inspired to volunteer to be of service in their school. Be prepared to offer them any references or credentials they want, and allow the time necessary for a trust relationship to develop. If you do commit to an activity or class, be very sure to honor that commitment. Doing so will make it easier for them to trust you and make it easier for the next man who wants to volunteer. If you have skills a school might use and the commitment, patience, and willingness to grow into the role, your presence as an adult male in a school setting will have a very important influence. You can be sure the boys in the school will be watching you very closely.

DeMolay

Another solid organization with a lot of man-making history is DeMolay. In 1919, a gentleman named Frank Land, who worked at the Scottish Rite Masonic Center in Kansas City, Missouri, was interviewing a young man, Louis Lower, for a position at the temple. Louis had made mention of how his father was killed in the war, and Mr. Land thought how sad it was that a boy should grow up without an adult man in his life. Mr. Land noted there were many such young men who had lost fathers due to the war. Soon after that conversation, Mr. Land asked Louis to invite several friends to their next meeting, with the purpose of starting a young men's fraternity. The Order of DeMolay was started and now has spread throughout the world.

DeMolay is an organization "dedicated to preparing young men to lead successful, happy, and productive lives..." and which strives to give boys civic awareness, personal responsibility, and the leadership skills that will help make them productive members of their communities. Membership is available to any young man aged twelve to twenty-one with good moral character. In more than a thousand chapters worldwide, DeMolay combines this serious mission with activities that are fun and which build relationships between boys and men. More than one million men have been involved with DeMolay at some point in their lives. Some of the more famous DeMolay alumni include Walt Disney, John Wayne, Walter Cronkite, football Hall-of-Famer Fran Tarkenton, legendary Nebraska football coach Tom Osborne, news anchor David Goodnow, and many others, including congressmen, military leaders, authors, musicians, and many other professionals. Even President Clinton was in DeMolay. Each of these men has spoken about the life-changing experiences that resulted from their involvement in this character-building organization.

One man with a solid connection to DeMolay is Joe. At forty-six, Joe has a man-making relationship with a young guy named Justin who was fourteen when Joe started dating Justin's mother, whom he later married. Joe explained that Justin had never had an adult male around him growing up. For most of his life, it was just him, his mom, and his grandmother. Because of his own experience with DeMolay, Joe thought DeMolay would be good for Justin and decided to take him to a meeting. Joe said, "I almost had to drag Justin to the first few meetings, but now when we go, he's out of the truck and on the run before I've even stopped. They have great 'young guy' activities such as go-carting, paintball, swimming, sledding, and other adventures. The contact with the other boys and men has brought Justin out of his shell and he's developing into a more confident young man."

While some of the boys involved in DeMolay have fathers who are connected to a Masonic organization, any boy can join. In fact, most boys in DeMolay don't have Masonic connections and the same is true for the adult volunteers. Today the organization openly welcomes boys and men with good moral character.

Joe is now an adult advisor with a local DeMolay chapter of about twenty boys, who Joe says, have that "know-it-all teen-age attitude." He says, "Being around them helps me to remember that age when I thought I knew everything. They are all very good kids, but they do need to be pointed in the right direction now and again. They run their own meetings and decide all the what, when, and how of their activities. The adults just offer advice when it's needed. The organization has great values, the boys are great, and working with other men is good for me. As Justin says, DeMolay is… 'a great place to learn guy stuff.'"

I have been associated with DeMolay over thirty-seven years, ever since I joined at age fourteen. The moral values, brotherhood and life skills learned have been instrumen-

tal in making me a better man, husband, father, professional, and citizen. I've gained lifelong friendships and
met DeMolay brothers all over the world in my travels.
DeMolay is closely tied to my successes, and because of
the close bond, I feel the need to give back so other young
men may gain, too, from the DeMolay experience.

Gary – 51

To learn more about the opportunities for your involvement with boys through DeMolay, visit the DeMolay website at
demolay.org to find a chapter near you.

Boys and Girls Clubs of America

The goal of the Boys and Girls Clubs of America (bgca.org) is to
develop boys (and starting in 1989, girls) into responsible adults.
The clubs serve children from all backgrounds, though special
consideration is given to those from disadvantaged circumstances.
Their mission is to "…help kids develop physically, mentally,
and emotionally by providing quality activities, emphasizing the
social skills necessary for each child to become an independent,
successful adult." The organization has an impressive alumni
list including such notables as Bill Cosby, Alex Rodriguez, Brad
Pitt, Michael Jordan, Bill Clinton, Jackie Joyner-Kersee, Martin
Sheen, Derek Jeter, Neil Diamond, and Denzel Washington.

One of club's offerings is Passport to Manhood, a man-making program available at many of the BGC locations. The program is specifically designed for middle-school boys who don't
have an adult male in their family life. To honor the boys in the
program, each Club participant receives his own "passport" to
underscore the notion that he is on a personal journey of matura-
tion and growth.

While the structure of the Passport to Manhood varies by
club, it often consists of small-group sessions that focus on a spe-

cific aspect of manhood through interactive discussions, activities, and in some places, meeting with local men who talk to them about topics such as family life, their professions, the military, and working in the trades. There is also the possibility of boy-driven discussions about whatever topic is hot for them that day as well as other topics of interest.

There just may be Boys and Girls Clubs in your city. If so, their Passport to Manhood program could really use your support and volunteer energy.

Helping Boys in Trouble

There is a very special form of volunteer man-making that's required for helping boys and young men who are in trouble. There are so many young males who, because of the absence of good (or any) parenting, and the lack of positive guidance from the adults around them, are creating problems in their communities. These lost boys are at very high risk for legal troubles or some other form of self-destruction.

The poem "Fatherless Son" is from contributor Ron Hepworth in New Zealand. It speaks to the sad story of a boy who is without his father and finds himself alone. In the poem, the boy is questioning the Ruru, a small owl native to New Zealand, which, in folklore, is considered the "twilight messenger that moves between the seen and the supernatural."

Fatherless Son

Old Ruru, tell me
    Where has my Father gone, I have no home
    I am empty and my world is cold

Wise Ruru
> *Can you sing me his songs, tell me his stories*
> *Show me the path that he walked*
>
> *Will you still my Mother's weeping, little Ruru*
> *Tell me .... what can I do?*

Child, said the feathered one, I knew him
> *For he worked the land, went down the mine,*
> *to the market place and ocean too*
>
> *But when he returned his home was empty*
> *And his children were not there*
>
> *In silent grief he stood; alone, outside the town*
> *and then, his song and dance were washed away*

Young one; it's too late to stop your Mother's tears
> *and I dare not say what will become of you*

A story from a young man named Dwayne has the same feel as the poem. Dwayne's story is typical of many thousands of young males who are lost to the streets, caught up in the legal system, or in jail. Many of these are young men who can be saved if the men around them become willing to get involved in their lives. Dwayne said, "My father passed away in 1996. I was a few months away from my eighteenth birthday and I was devastated. He had been a heavy drinker, hard-hearted and was rough around the edges, but he was my hero.

"With my dad gone, I lived in a house dominated by females and female interests and things often got frustrating. My older brother was making a life for himself in the Navy and was living many miles away. I had no man I was directly under, and no mature male presence to help me feel good about myself.

"Fed up with the home scene, I ventured out into the streets and hung out with others my age. On the street there were people for me to look up to, I had independence and felt like a man. I drank my own liquor, smoked my own cigarettes and weed, and even carried a gun. On the street, people didn't argue with me every day. People didn't insult me because I did bad in school. On the street, I felt I was respected and had a sense of belonging.

"But I was vulnerable for shaping into any form. As a result, I got caught up in gang violence and wound up in prison till I was twenty-one. The rest is a long, hard story, but my point is that if my hero, my dad, had understood the value of being a responsible man and raising a son, he might not have died and left me father-less and confused."

The number of boys incarcerated in jails, detention boot camps, treatment facilities, halfway houses, or placement homes, just breaks my heart. Boys in trouble with the law are especially in need of the attention of older men. Because of their emotional wounds and usually negative history with the men in their lives, it can be especially difficult to build and then maintain ongoing relationships. If you have the courage to do front-line work in the struggle to save our boys, helping boys in trouble is a great way to apply your man-making energies. You can contact any branch of law enforcement in your community and you'll quickly find out where you might step into service in support of the young males in the juvenile justice system.

> I've been a field social worker for the County for the last twenty years. In that role, I've been a part of the journey to young adulthood for countless numbers of both boys and girls from age twelve to twenty-one. While these kids come from every part of our community, many of them are involved with the juvenile justice system and have deep personal issues. It's not easy work, but the gifts I get from working with these kids always seem to more than compensate for the challenges involved. I guarantee that anyone who makes a commitment to these kids will get plenty of good things in return.
>
> Jim J. – 55

One group of New Jersey men, affiliated with the Man Kind Project (MKP), found a creative way to support troubled boys. MKP is a man-making program for adult men, with centers throughout the United States, and in Canada, Australia, South Africa, and England. Its stated purpose is, ". . . to create a safer world by growing better men." You can learn more about this organization at the mkp.org website. Involvement with MKP begins with a New Warrior Training Adventure weekend, which is followed up with participation in an ongoing Integration Group.

An Integration Group, or I-group, of men from New Jersey figured out how to "adopt" a residence for very challenged young males. The residence houses boys from thirteen to eighteen years old who have been abandoned, abused, let down by their families, or gotten in trouble with the law. The staff at the residence was looking for positive male role models who could befriend and guide their boys and the MKP men stepped forward. Greg, one of the MKP men, describes how the adventure unfolded.

At our first meeting of the I-group men and boys, there were fifteen men and sixteen boys. It started with pizza and getting to know each other and then naturally led to questions and sharing of opinions and experiences. That first meeting exceeded everyone's expectations and has since evolved into monthly meetings and many positive relationships for both men and boys.

Now, when we meet, the combined group engages in a variety of activities like building things, making recordings of the boys' rap music, writing poetry, learning how to play pool, and even mastering the yo-yo.

Our major role is just to be with the boys, listen to them, show them who we are, share what we think, and demonstrate, by our presence, that we care about them. We sometimes look at ourselves kind of as the boys' uncles or older brothers. For boys who have been abandoned repeatedly, having men who show up consistently and demonstrate an interest in them has a very powerful impact on their lives.

Should you, or you and some of your men friends, choose to volunteer at any of the many places troubled boys are confined, you'll need open hearts, lots of patience, and you can be sure your commitment will be seriously tested. Because of the overload of work and under-funding, the people working with boys in these situations may not have a lot of time for training. As a result, like the men from the MKP group, you may have to use your courage, creativity, and on-the-job training to learn your way into the boys' hearts.

As the MKP men reported, the experience is "unbelievably rewarding for both the boys and all the men involved." You may even discover the answer to a question asked of the MKP men by one of the boys in the group home. At the close of one of their evening meetings, the young guy asked the men, "What took you guys so long to get here?"

• • • • •

Regardless of how you choose to get involved as a volunteer man-maker with a group of boys, once you do, you'll experience that special kind of exchange between you and the boys that the men in these examples have been describing. You will clearly see the difference in boys' lives that results from your consistent presence. You'll understand that you've become very important in their lives, and for some boys, critically important.

If you feel you want a more in-depth relationship with a boy, you may want to consider the extra time and effort involved in a one-on-one relationship. In the next chapter, you'll learn about the many possibilities that exist for one-man-one-boy relationships, and the different set of rewards waiting for you there.

5

One-on-One
Man-Making

I had an amazing adventure when I was very young, maybe nine. I went with our neighbor Mark and his kids to "the tower." The Highland Park water tower was a ten-storey stone structure built in the 1920s at the highest point in St. Paul, Minnesota, to create water pressure for the community. As they did back then, the builders created an artistic as well as a functional structure, with an internal stairway for reaching the viewing platform at the very top. After our long, clanging haul up the metal stairs in the musty darkness, we finally burst out into the sunlight at the top.

My first sensation, never having been that far up in the sky, was that I could literally see to the edge of the earth. A 360-degree panorama allowed me to see parts of the planet I never knew existed. Mark took each of us in turn, lifted us up on his knee, and patiently pointed out our homes, the movie theater, our school, and other places we'd only heard about. That day, my perspective and understanding of my world grew significantly.

What Mark was doing is at the heart of man-making. It is lifting a boy's self-esteem and helping him to see a new and larger view of his world. It means taking the time to help a boy understand how things in the larger landscape connect and fit together and showing him how the world looks from an older man's perspective. Once mentored in this way, a boy's understanding of his relationship with the world and his rightful place in the order of things is forever changed.

All of the different man-making roles you have been learning about are enormously helpful and necessary for a boy's journey to manhood. Yet there are some things a boy can get only from a more personal, focused, and enduring relationship with an adult man. Geoff Price, co-founder of the Pathways Foundation in Australia (and author of *Puberty Boy)*, is correct when he says, "How can a boy become a healthy man if he has never spent time with a man up close? A boy needs the presence and active involvement of an older man. My experience is that telling boys how to be a man doesn't work. Men need to allow boys to be around them so the boys can soak up manhood."

In this chapter, we'll explore two different approaches to one-on-one man-making. I call the first form of connection Informal Man-Making. It refers to the casual relationships that more or less happen between men and young males. These connections are comfortable because they are based on mutual affinity, vary greatly in their duration, and have little or no formal structure. It's the role that my neighbor Mark was playing in my life when he took me to the watertower. They more or less just happen.

The second form of one-on-one connection I call Intentional Man-Making. It's when a man decides he wants to make a positive difference in a young man's life and intentionally signs on, usually with a mentoring organization, to be matched with a young guy who also wants an older man in his life. These matches are most often for a specified period of time, have a structured schedule for being together, and offer lots of organization support for both participants.

Let's begin by looking at Informal Man-Making and what researchers call Natural Mentors.

Informal Man-Making

Unfortunately, in too many families today, the boys' fathers are gone, distant, unavailable, or just not interested. In those cases, the best thing that can happen is a man from the boy's family or another interested man will come forward to become a one-on-one man-maker in his life. These informal relationships can and often do evolve naturally as the boy's relatives, friends of the family, neighbors, men from the boy's spiritual community, other boys' fathers, or even the guy at the local store see what's needed and step up.

The first group of informal man-makers I'd like to discuss are a boy's male relatives, the male members of his "family tribe." If these men can see the opportunity, they can have an enormously positive influence in a boy's life. It's in their blood so to speak, IF they get it!

A Boy's Male Relatives

Down through history, it wasn't the boy's father who initiated his son into manhood. That was the job of the boy's male relatives and the other men of the tribe. Because of that history, a boy is set up for his biological uncles and grandfathers to have a natural role to play on the boy's journey to manhood. These men have the advantages of knowing the family dynamics and having a history with the boy, and they often live close by. Because of an adolescent boy's tendency to test limits, there can be hurt feelings, pent-up frustration, and a lack of trust between a boy and his parents. Uncles and grandfathers are on the outside of that grind of daily family life. If they are willing and available, these men can often support a boy in ways that simply aren't available to parents.

My dad wasn't around so I was really raised by my
uncle. He was like a father to me. He taught me how

to fish, hunt, use a bow, and all that guy stuff. I learned about his job and other life stuff when I was with him. We moved two states away from him and now I only see him on holidays. I try to see him every chance I get. I really miss him.

Mike – 18

Time with an uncle or grandfather is rarely about discipline or managing boy behavior. These men typically don't have a big agenda about how their nephew or grandson should behave, so they can just enjoy him for who he is. These connections can be playful, interesting, supportive, and even irreverent. Being with an older male family member is a time-honored way for a boy to get a different perspective on himself and all the benefits that come with hanging out with a cool male elder. One contributor, Doug, shared how an uncle can be an enormous gift to a boy's parents.

My involvement with my brother's oldest son started when he began seriously abusing drugs. My brother felt powerless, didn't know what to do, and welcomed my involvement with his son. I organized a chemical dependency intervention and we got him into a treatment program in my hometown. I visited him several times while he was in the program and have stayed in close touch with him ever since. We talk about once a month and I see him a couple times a year when I get to his state. He is doing okay, seems to be straight, and relies on me to the proper degree.

In helping him through this process, I feel I was doing what a caring family member should do, and what his father, in spite of his love for his son, couldn't do. I'm thrilled the intervention was successful and that my nephew has his life back on track.

Family Gatherings

A boy's male relatives have some unique man-making opportunities when families gather on the big holidays, at weddings, and at funerals. In addition to the focus of the event, when your clan gathers, it's a great time to simply engage your young male relatives in conversation. Standing around the edges of these activities is where shy boys, uncles, and grandfathers tend to hang out anyway.

Family gatherings are the perfect time to connect with your young relative, learn a little about his life, tell him some family stories, and introduce him to other members of your larger family. This will help the boy to learn he's part of a clan with a history that goes back farther than he may realize. He'll discover people who vaguely resemble him and talk like him, and he'll be able to hear interesting stories about where he's come from and what his ancestors did. This experience creates an important sense of belonging for the young man and will help him feel connected to something bigger than his immediate family. You may even find the connections you make at these gatherings will grow into more involved relationships over time.

It was at my father's funeral that I was introduced to the man I came to call my Uncle Richard. Because of the family politics, I never even knew he existed until my dad's funeral. He was actually my father's uncle and my great-uncle, but because he was the youngest in his family, at seventy-nine, he was at the perfect elder age for me.

I really don't enjoy any food that contains over-cooked celery. My Uncle Richard, on the other hand, loved going out to lunch for chow mein, a dish full of the mushy green vegetable. I think he knew I wasn't wild about the food, and to tease me he'd begin each of these meals with an incantation about how difficult it was to "get good chow mein these days." Aside from that small limitation, our shared mealtimes were full of stories about my family I'd never heard. I learned the details of how my grandfather Earl died on a motorcycle on a rainy day when he hit the wet streetcar tracks, and the one about when Uncle Richard and my father hopped freight cars to travel around the country to look for work during the Depression. For me, Uncle Richard was a fat history book stuffed full of interesting information about my family that was all fascinating to me.

Most importantly, Uncle Richard was the only adult male in my whole extended family who really took an interest in the details of my life. He went out of his way to hang out with me, he was capable of saying he was proud of me, and he regularly told me he loved me. It is one of the tragedies of my life that I didn't discover this man until five years before his death. I'm still mad at the forces that kept my extended family angry at each other, disconnected, and distant for so long. I wanted, deserved, and needed a clan. Still, I'm grateful for Uncle Richard. He enriched my life immeasurably for five wonderful years.

Elder Blessing

Another important man-making role for an adult male is to honor and bless your adolescent male relatives at important times in their lives. Events such as birthdays, graduations, getting school awards, or the happy, yet frightening, day a boy gets his permit to drive, can each be sufficient reason for you to honor him or even to gather a few of his older male friends and relatives around him for acknowledgement, maybe some advice-giving, and celebration. It's in an adolescent boy's job description to resist this spotlighting, but whether it's a family celebration or just the two of you recognizing one of his achievements, deep down he will love it. It may also just become a habit for you, leading to a wonderful relationship with the young man.

Natural Mentors

Not all boys are lucky enough to have family members show up for them. That is why the other men of the village, if they get it, are needed to support young males. These connections are often naturally occurring, and can be initiated by either the younger or older male. Sometimes men don't even realize they are having an influence (for better or worse) on the young men around them.

> I never had any living grandfathers and no geographically close uncles. I was raised by she-wolves. But if I dig deep, I can remember one important man. His name was Harry, an African American man (in those days Negro) who stopped for a time in the small, white, Western town where we lived.
>
> My dad was a travelling salesman and on the road a great deal. My mom ran a small deli with the help of my grandmother. I guess Harry just happened by and needed work.
>
> I remember him as a kind, gentle, and patient man who did odd jobs. I vaguely remember following him around, observing and having conversations. I don't remember many of the details, but he was interested in me. The recalling of this small memory stirs something in me, which I can't identify and only recognize in the tears I am experiencing at this moment.
>
> Steve – 60

> I have a great, long-term relationship with a young guy named Tyler. It began when he was eight years old. I was having a conversation with a friend of mine and mentioned I was considering becoming a man-maker for some young guy. Without skipping a beat, she suggested talking to the single woman who lived next door to her who had three kids. The mom had been pregnant with her youngest boy, Tyler, when her husband suddenly died

nine years ago, so Tyler had never had an adult male in his life. My friend thought Tyler was a great kid and that his mom would be open to the idea.

As it turns out, my friend was right. Our connection has resulted in years of hanging out together and me getting to watch Tyler grow into a fine young man. It was an informal connection that wouldn't have happened if I hadn't spoken my intention to become a man-maker.

Most men, when they look back on their lives, will realize that during their developmental years, they either consciously or unconsciously adopted older men. These adopted men may not even have realized they were being targeted and emulated. In some cases, close or at least important relationships developed. Each adult man brought a different set of gifts and challenges to the emerging young male. In this way, young men instinctively construct their own *male tribe*... an unconsciously created circle of older men, each of whom carries a piece of manhood worthy of emulation. If men are lucky, this process of collecting male guides will continue throughout their lives as their journey to manhood continues.

When I first met Art, my boss, he intimidated the hell out of me. He was tough, aggressive, and demanding and had a reputation for hammering people for not performing. He wasn't afraid to take on the really hard assignments and he was the guy that people went to when they had a difficult problem or a tough project. People respected him and he made me work my ass off. Art persuaded me to go back to school to get my mechanical engineering degree (I graduated with honors). This was after a high school guidance counselor had told me I should consider a vocational school because I wasn't ever going to amount to much. My life changed through my relationship with Art, and I'll never forget him.

Barry – 45

Recent research from the University of Illinois at Chicago, published in the *American Journal of Public Health*, speaks to the value of what the researchers call natural mentors. David DuBois, lead author of the study, says, "Unlike mentors who are assigned by a program, natural mentors come from different areas of the young person's own life such as their extended family, neighbors, teachers, coaches, religious leaders and employers." Using data from the National Longitudinal Study of Adolescent Health, the researchers found more than 70% of those in the study reported a natural mentoring relationship with an adult, and that these relationships lasted an average of nine years. The study found that a young person with a natural mentor had:

- a greater likelihood of completing high school, attending college, and working at least ten hours per week;
- a decreased likelihood of being in a gang and having physically hurt someone in a fight in the past year, as well as a lower level of risk-taking;
- higher levels of self-esteem and life satisfaction;
- a greater level of physical activity, as well as regular use of birth control.

While many of these informal and natural man-making relationships extend over long periods of time, occasionally a brief encounter with a caring adult male, at just the right moment, can be life-shaping for a young man. Forty-four-year-old Paul remembered a brief interaction with a friend of his family named Herb.

It was summer and I was living at home with my parents before heading into my senior year of college. My dad mentioned a family friend, Herb, had a set of tires that just might fit my 1965 Ford Galaxy 500. Herb and his son had been on a couple of hunting trips with Dad and me over the years and I felt comfortable with him. I drove over to check on the tires but it turned out they weren't the right size. Walking back to my car, Herb started asking me some typical adult questions like how is college going and what did I plan to do when I was done? The more questions I answered the more he asked. We talked over two hours as we leaned against my car in the driveway.

I don't think Herb was aware of just how powerful that brief interaction came to be in my life. In the course of that conversation, I found clarification of my goals and dreams, and a sense of being treated as an adult with valid ambitions and the ability to forge my own path. His confidence in me, objective questioning, and sincere interest in what I had to say helped to shape the decisions I made over the next several years of my life.

If you are open to the possibility of an informal, one-on-one connection with an adolescent male, and you're paying attention to the young men around you, it won't be long before a natural man-making possibility presents itself. In fact, I'm sure a boy is already circling you, waiting to be seen.

Whether you "discover" a young man, or he finds you, don't be surprised when you find yourself in an informal man-making relationship. Because it will most likely be a "natural" connection, you can trust you'll have everything you'll need by way of talking points and ideas for hang time. But in case you'd like some extra inspiration, what follows are descriptions of a variety of informal, one-on-one man-making activities you and your young pal can sample.

These examples are offered mostly to help you with any fear you might have about not knowing what to do. If you're like most natural mentors, once your relationship is rolling, "what to do" will naturally emerge out of a little creativity and your time together.

Fixing Things

A perfect man-making area is the whole world of tools, construction, and home repair. Do-it-yourself projects require the use of tools, learning how to find your way around the mysterious, yet fascinating, aisles of a hardware store, and learning how to think through a project in an orderly way. Inviting an adolescent male to help on a project, hold tools, and give his opinion along the way, is sure to engage his interest. In addition, if you're like me and weren't taught basic construction or home repair skills, the young man will most likely pick up some questionable language for expressing frustration in the process.

Fixing appliances, repairing plumbing, and seeing how things work by taking them apart and putting them back together are all great ways to capture a young male's attention. I love to take a young guy to *my* Home Depot. These giant hardware stores, with their garage-like appearance, parts of things hanging on the walls, tools everywhere, and forklift trucks running around, make them feel like veritable temples of secret guy knowledge. For a young male who hasn't been exposed to that kind of place, just walking around can be a serious male adventure.

If you are handy with tools, enjoy repairing things, and are interested in a connection with boys, you can quickly become a powerful man-maker just by having a boy help you fix a toilet, a light switch, or a faucet. Even if you have to run out in the middle of the project to get some advice, you'll still be teaching the boy a man doesn't have to know everything, and asking for help when you're stuck is a successful strategy. I wish I'd gotten that lesson earlier! A fifty-three-year-old man, named Cris, speaks to the man-making power in these seemingly simple acts of construction.

Young boys tend to be kinesthetic learners and doing things with their hands really helps their learning process. Showing a young man how to use tools and working with his hands to translate thoughts and ideas into three-dimensional objects is almost a spiritual journey. If this act of creation happens often enough, a bond is formed between the boy and a man that is as strong as any bond in a young man's life. To see how a young man can hold an older male in such awe is well worth any effort I expend to make those moments happen. Interested men, boys, tools, and construction materials make for endless possibilities.

Just Doing Stuff

What my young pal Tyler and I really loved about the St. Paul Saints, a minor league baseball team in a major league town, was how they used a small pig wearing a little backpack to take fresh baseballs out to the pitcher. The Saints are always trying to keep the game experience fun and interesting. They have a theme for each game, zany competitions, fun events between each inning, and even a Jacuzzi hot tub in the far left field stands where four or so fans can watch the game in their bathing suits.

Tyler and I were heading for a game on a summer afternoon and as we approached the gates, people were being asked to sign up to lead a treasure hunt in their section. Tyler didn't want to do it, but I explained that taking the occasional risk and trying new things often has big rewards. The short story is that Tyler and I won the treasure hunt. I won a three-thousand-dollar diamond ring for my wife and Tyler got a game ball and a new glove. When I asked Tyler the lesson in that experience, he put it very simply, "do stuff." Since that day, whenever he's been a little reluctant to try something new, I just say, "Remember, do stuff." Since then, Tyler's used that line on me more than once.

If there is an adolescent male in your neighborhood, consider inviting him to do stuff. Going to a baseball game is great, but "doing stuff" together doesn't have to mean spending an extended amount of time together or even going on an exciting adventure. Outings of any kind help the two of you connect and create an opening for offhand, easy-going, side-by-side guy communication. Even mundane activities like going walking, shopping at the mall, buying groceries, seeing a movie, playing miniature golf, taking a trip to the hardware store, or visiting friends, all have value for a young man. In all of these activities, a boy can watch an older male in action, learn how he thinks, and notice what commands his attention. Following men around is one of the ways boys have always used to learn how to be men. Don't underestimate the lessons for a boy when you take him on the less-than-glamorous, small adventures, and *just do stuff.*

Sharing Hobbies

I have a fledgling interest in rock climbing. In our community, we have an REI sporting goods store with an indoor climbing wall set up near the entrance. I first took a young friend, Okun, to try out the wall when he was about nine. He was fascinated by the "mountain," special shoes, the safety harness, carabiners, all the ropes, and the notion of belaying someone for safety.

When his turn came to climb the wall, Okun was so wired he literally scampered through the first dozen or so moves. Then, at about three-quarters of the way up, he looked down and scared the crap out of himself. Suddenly, Okun's arms started to weaken, his legs started to shake, and the excuses started to fly. Shortly thereafter, my young friend stalled out completely. I yelled a compliment up to him saying I was impressed he'd gotten that far and suggested he'd accomplished a lot for the first time out. After that blessing, Okun, with pride intact, happily rappelled down.

Okun showed a lot of courage for a first-timer, had fun with some new gear, and faced a huge challenge. After that first experience on the REI climbing wall, we've gone back almost yearly as one of our traditions. We've both enjoyed how, over time, that *mountain* appears to get smaller and smaller. Okun came along for the ride on my interest and had a great experience. He did get even, however, by taking me for a ride on his interest. It turns out the young dude loves BIG roller coasters. In the name of fair play, I've almost puked a couple times on a huge roller coaster called "Wild Thing" that's Okun's favorite—but it was fun!

Whether your hobbies include flying airplanes, orienteering, collecting coins, studying maps, studying a language, making clay pots, playing chess, drag racing at the track, or any of a million other activities, take the risk to share them with a young male. You never can tell what will result. Greg Z. is fifty-six and was volunteering at a correctional facility for young men when he encountered a seventeen-year-old black man named Leon. Greg tells the story of the surprise he experienced when he took a large risk to share his interest in poetry with Leon.

> Leon had been in and out of correctional institutions for more than half his short life. Standing about five-feet, ten inches, weighing a very muscular one hundred and eighty pounds, and often exhibiting a brooding attitude, Leon presented an almost menacing appearance. I suggested I might be able to visit on weekends and he liked the idea, so we began.
>
> I enjoy writing poetry and have some skill at it. At first, I hesitated to bring that up to Leon, but when I finally did, I realized I had misjudged him. Leon had been writing poetry for years. When I showed him a couple of techniques I used, he took to them very well and wrote some very good pieces. Our mutual love of poetry has become an important connection between us.

If you begin a man-making relationship around an activity you enjoy, it makes the relationship more interesting for both you and the young man. It's safe to say that once you start following each other's interests, you'll have an amazing array of possible activities that are guaranteed to keep your relationship evolving.

Showing Up

The most important man-making activity in a one-on-one relationship is to show up at the important times in a boy's life. When Tyler was in his early teens and performing in his high school plays, I'd attend whenever possible. Because of the social chaos at these events, I'd rarely get to talk with him. However, when he was on stage I could see him scanning the theater to see if his friends and family were there. When I'd see him looking my way I'd give him a little wave, but he was way too cool at that age to actually acknowledge my presence. I'd usually call him later in the week to talk about the play and how well he did. Though he rarely said anything by way of appreciation, it was clear in our conversation he was pleased to have an older guy in his life who enjoyed watching him and always had something good to say about his performances.

A forty-five-year-old man named Steve describes the feelings that commonly result for both parties in a man-making relationship when the older man "shows up." Steve loves baseball, has coached in the past, and is a real student of the game. Derek was the seventeen-year-old son of Steve's friend and a sophomore starter on a high school varsity team. In fine man-making tradition, Steve began showing up for Derek's games. He tells this story about his experience.

> I made a few long treks out to see him play and I could tell he really appreciated that I made the effort.

Derek's parents and grandparents are very involved, but I could tell my being there and not being family really meant something to him. Last year I went to six or seven of his baseball games. Each time I'd see him look over and acknowledge me. After the games he'd come up to me to thank me for making the game. He'd even listen to my advice about his plays. He liked me being there and it made me feel good. I know he's not my son, but I can still feel proud. And I do.

Whether it's sporting events, graduations, school plays, recitals, or supporting him by buying a holiday wreath or candy for his school's fund-raisers, just showing up for the important events in a young man's life is unbelievably important. Your simple presence says you care about him, he's valuable enough to get your time, and that he counts in the eyes of an older guy. Those actions may not seem like much to you, but for a boy who is starving for adult male attention, it means so very much.

Getting the Meat

I remember a story I read about a boy shooting his first deer. After the boy's kill, his grandfather cut open the deer's belly and put his hands in the still-warm guts. He removed his bloody hands and smeared the deer's blood on the boy's face. This was a powerful initiation ritual: a statement about the boy's accomplishment and the bond between the boy and the deer. It was such a potent and primitive image that I have never forgotten it. Getting the meat is something men have always done, and being seen as *man enough* to go with the men to hunt is what boys have always wanted.

No one in my family was a hunter, so I didn't get exposure to hunting as a kid. I heard about friends shooting their first deer, but all my in-the-woods adventure stories are about mosquitoes and just-about-perfect marshmallows falling in the fire. If you enjoy hunting or fishing, these adventures can lead to high-quality man-making time because they reek of masculinity. Hunting and fishing can involve men and boys being together in the natural world, sometimes with a degree of danger—stalking prey, using knives and other gear, building fires, and lots of sitting-around time. For a boy, these activities are wild, seemingly dangerous, and full of adventure, even if you're just going ten miles from home and don't bring anything home but stories and memories. Cole, who is now fifty-four, describes the desire he had to join the generations of men in his family who had a cherished hunting tradition.

> My dad and Uncle George were both hunters. They would travel to Idaho, where my grandfather owned some land and liked to hunt elk. They hunted on horseback, as a team of men using pack animals. I can remember my dad going off to hunt with the "men" and, even though I wasn't old enough, I still asked if I could join them. I asked because it was for the MEN and I wanted to go.

At a certain point in a young male's life, he desperately wants to join the men in this age-old tradition. It is, after all, wired into a boy's genes. Everything about him—his new physical strength, his desire for an active adventure with a male tribe, and his emerging sense of personal power—has him primed for the hunt. Most of all, he wants the recognition from older men that says, "OK, you are now man enough to join us."

When I was about nine years old, I had my first look inside my neighbor Mark's old green metal tackle box. Fishing line, multi-colored lures, hooks, feathers, sinkers, spinners, red-and-white bobbers, knives... that box contained a whole universe of tools I didn't know existed. It had a haunting, but compelling, fragrance I now know was twenty years' accumulation of dried fish guts and pieces of leeches and worms, all seasoned with a little beer. For me, looking into that box was opening a door to a secret and exciting male universe. I wanted to know what each item was, how to use it, and the magic it would create. Mark patiently explained each lure, the fish it attracted, and how to fish with each one. He further stirred my interest by talking about catching the "big ones," and what it took to land them. Mark and I did eventually go fishing, but that adventure all began with our exploring the contents of that old tackle box.

While hunting and fishing are usually good, one-on-one man-making activities, they aren't for every boy. Some will find the idea of shooting a gun, baiting a hook, killing an animal, or being in the wilderness just too frightening or unappealing. You may connect with a young guy through an interest in simply tracking animals, going birding, or the skill of orienteering. These are all ways to be out in the natural world, using gear, and finding your way around without doing harm to living creatures.

If you do hunt or fish, you might see if some young man might want to tag along. You can get a sense of his degree of interest by simply talking about the activity or going shopping for the gear. That will allow the boy's curiosity to cook for a while. Seeing the equipment and hearing the stories of the "big one that got away" will often speak to a boy's dormant hunter genes. Because "getting the meat" is an ancient man-boy activity and hardwired into our male brains, your skills at these kinds of sports are sure to inspire a degree of awe in a boy somewhere in your life.

Learning to Drive

In today's world, there are few rites of passage for a young man that compare with the freedom and status that come with a license to drive. If there is a young man of your acquaintance who has reached the age when a driver's license is in sight, you can become his hero by volunteering to teach him how to drive. The boy's parents will be eternally grateful because they know they won't have the patience for the job. For many parents, just the thought of their adolescent with driving rights is so frightening, it's often put off until the last possible minute or until they give their kids over to a driver's education instructor. If you have parental support, hopefully their car, and nerves of steel, teaching a boy to drive is a natural opportunity for some great man-making.

Assuming your young man has passed the preliminary tests and has all the right credentials, you and he can drive off to some remote location and instruction can commence. You can question him about the rules of the road, talk about what to do in different driving scenarios, and teach the important manual skills that will increase both his mastery and, hopefully, his respect for the lethal power of two-plus tons of metal moving at high speed.

In this man-making action, you'll not only be establishing a connection with the young man, but you may be literally saving his life. The data is clear that young male drivers, those who are sixteen and seventeen, have three times the accidents their slightly older male peers do. Guiding a young man into this complicated world of driving skills and responsibilities is a very important man-making activity. In addition, the anxiety you're sure to experience, and the certain fumbling on the boy's part, are sure to result in some great stories you'll both be laughing about for years to come.

• • • • •

Of all the forms of man-making, it's the longer-term, one-on-one connection between a boy and an adult man that is the most life-shaping for both males. As a man named Gene found out, an informal, natural mentoring relationship can endure and powerfully shape the lives of both of the guys:

I was a sort of uncle to a boy named Tony from the time he was seven until he was fourteen. I got involved with him because of my relationship with his mom. Tony's dad had left the family, leaving Tony without adequate supervision and a good male role model. As a result, he was getting very unruly. A number of times he'd simply leave his classes, and he was expelled from school more than once. Tony was one of those kids who loved guns, had no friends, and was headed for trouble.

With his mom's blessing, Tony and I started hanging out one evening a week. We'd eat at McDonald's, go shopping, see a movie, take in a special event, or just spend time at home. Over time, Tony and I developed a close relationship, and his behavior began to improve. We both came to look forward to our weekly get-togethers.

I doubt if there's a direct correlation, but he loved rock music and over the years, I bought him a number of CDs. Today Tony is a successful disc jockey in Oregon. While my time with him was relatively short, I've gained so much, knowing that I had a real impact on this one boy's life. I think I really filled a blank for Tony at a time when an older male influence was critical. I'm just very proud of what he has become.

Gene – 75

Informal one-on-one man-making relationships, that evolve naturally over time, are the most common form of man-making. However, if you want to start having an immediate and direct impact in a boy's life, you can do that through a variety of organizations that set up official one-man, one-boy relationships. I call that intentional man-making.

Intentional Man-Making

Connections with young guys, offered through mentoring organizations, are a great way to step into man-making. It just so happens that in almost every community there are lots of one-on-one, mentoring organizations that would love your involvement. Let's briefly explore a couple of ways you can connect with these groups and become an official man-maker.

The National Mentoring Partnership

In my home state there is an organization called the Mentoring Partnership of Minnesota (mentoringworks.org) which is a member of MENTOR/National Mentoring Partnership (mentoring.org). The Minnesota organization works with more than 400 organizations throughout the state that promote mentoring. They say, at any given moment in time, somewhere around 75,000 Minnesota kids are waiting for a mentoring relationship. Because of this severe shortage of mentors, *every day*, requests by kids to be put on a *waiting list* for a mentor are turned down. The same situation is most likely occurring in your part of the world.

In the U.S.A., the MENTOR/National Mentoring Partnership website (mentoring.org) will direct you to organizations looking for mentors in thirty different states. A quick search by zip code will turn up organizations in your area that have opportunities waiting for you. Most of them will do background checking, provide some training, offer guidelines for involvement, have suggestions for activities, have parent support, and provide advisors. Once you're connected to a mentoring organization, you'll have the benefit of interaction with other men who have been at it for a while. If it's time to step into a one-on-one relationship, any of the mentoring organizations near you will love to get your call.

Big Brothers Big Sisters

While there are many hundreds of mentoring-based organizations, Big Brothers Big Sisters (bbbsa.org) is the one we most commonly think of for one-boy, one-man relationships. This organization is more than a hundred years old, is international in its reach, and has a great track record for matching kids with adult mentors/friends. According to their research, the statistics for youth involved in Big Brothers Big Sisters indicate involved kids are 46% less likely to use illegal drugs, 27% less likely to begin using alcohol, and 52% less likely to skip school. In addition, kids with a Big Brother or Big Sister are more confident in their performance at school, one-third less likely to hit someone, and more trusting of their parents/guardians. That's a nice return for a small investment of time.

Big Brothers Big Sisters provides every possible support for the volunteer mentors (Bigs), parents, and the kids being mentored (Littles). With its history, resources, and community recognition, Big Brothers Big Sisters would be a very good place to start your man-making adventure.

At a time when he was looking for some way to help his community, a fifty-four-year-old contributor named Mark talked to some men who were official Big Brothers, got inspired, and signed on. In the process, Mark learned about the challenges and the rewards that came with being a Big Brother to a ten-year-old boy named Kenny. Kenny's mother and grandmother were both prostitutes and his father was in prison. Once he got involved, Mark said he quickly began to understand his man-making potential.

> I got a strong sense I was contributing something important to Kenny's life. For example, I brought him to our apartment many times, so he could see what a more normal life looked like. While I often felt frustrated by my inability to get through to Kenny, he always felt we were

doing fine. I'm certain he liked all the attention although he'd never say so. After my wife and I moved, I lost track of Kenny. I just hope I was one of the lights along the way that lit up his path to a different way of life.

Few one-on-one man-making relationships are anywhere near as challenging as the relationship Mark had with Kenny. You can be sure if you intentionally move into man-making through a structured program like Big Brothers Big Sisters, or any of the other similar programs, you will get all the help and support you'll need to have a positive experience. Like Mark, you will very quickly become an important part of a young man's life. Once you get past the initial stages or relationship building, you'll discover you really are hardwired for this important form of relationship. Very soon your connection will feel natural, comfortable, and enormously rewarding.

e-Mentoring

If you're not ready for face-to-face involvement, you can make a big difference in a boy's life from your home computer. "e-Mentoring" is the name most commonly used for programs that match school kids with adults from local businesses and community organizations for e-mail academic tutoring.

The e-Mentoring model is simple. One student is matched with one mentor. Teachers provide specific assignments that direct the e-mail communications between the mentor and student. The students and mentors exchange weekly e-mails on the topic and may also have occasional phone or face-to-face meetings for one-on-one tutoring. At the completion of the curriculum, there is usually a closure activity and a celebration of accomplishment.

This is the perfect solution for busy adults who want to contribute something to their community by helping a student, and for young people who really need the academic coaching and a supportive adult in their lives. While the physical distance is greater than an in-person connection, solid and sometimes long-term relationships develop between students and mentors. Teachers give the program high marks, and sponsoring employers see benefits to volunteer employees.

It may take some digital searching, but there is most likely an e-mentoring program somewhere in your community. If you're comfortable in the world of e-mail, this is an elegant yet simple way to make a big difference in a young person's life and to get started in a mentoring relationship.

The One-on-One Man-Making Job Description

Being a man-maker in a one-on-one relationship is really quite easy because you only have to be yourself and show up regularly in a boy's life. It's a time to be relaxed, to get to know each other, listen to each other's opinions about things, have some fun, shoot the crap, learn from each other, do some interesting stuff, and just hang out. As in any evolving relationship, you may have to work through any issues in the way of the two of you getting along. However, once the relationship is established, it's mostly about having a fun, safe, interesting, intergenerational, male friendship. Frans, a forty-four-year-old man from the Netherlands, describes exactly how these relationships work.

> I'm forty-four and my partner is forty. We really like children, but we've made a conscious choice not to have our own. A very good friend of ours has a son named Steven, who's ten now. His parents divorced when he was four years old. With his parents' approval, Steven and I have a lot of fun together. We are learning to play guitar

together and we're restoring a twenty-year-old moped. Last week we did a little plumbing. He really liked using the blowtorch and working with the tin-lead solder. We are both looking forward to riding my motorcycle this coming spring. When we're together, we just have fun. Sometimes a boy needs an older man in his life and sometimes I like to have a young boy in mine.

As the stories you've been reading indicate, many man-making relationships between men and boys are casual, unstructured, and intermittent. This is in large part how guys create relationships. Yet a man with a firm commitment and just a little training can easily become a more influential man-maker in a one-on-one connection. If you're teetering on the edge of involvement in a one-man-one-boy relationship, the following guidelines should help you resolve any lingering fears or concerns. Think of this as a one-on-one man-making job description. It starts right at the beginning of the new relationship.

Get Parental Blessing

In any ongoing man-making relationship, you'll want to be sure you have parental blessing and support for your activities. As part of the package, you're going to be in a relationship with one or both parents. Obviously, a son is precious to them and, if the boy is lucky, his parents will be concerned and have questions about you. Early on in the relationship, when trust is still building, if it's at all possible, meet the boy's parents. Let them get to know you, tell them about your life, your family, and most importantly, your motivations for hanging out with their son.

It's very reasonable for the parents to want some references on you. If they ask, give them the names and contact information for you and your family members, your employer, your neighbors, a contact in your spiritual community, or any other information that might help them see that you and your intentions are trustworthy. Most organizations that establish official mentoring relationships also do some form of background check. When you provide the same information, it will help to put the parents at ease.

You can also ask them questions about their son, his history, and their hopes for your relationship with him. They can give you important information about the boy's likes and dislikes, and support your relationship with their son. Initially, you may even want to include them when it comes to making decisions about some of your activities.

Most parents, and especially single mothers, instinctively recognize the gifts for their son in a relationship with a good man. Once parents get to know and trust you, they will most likely welcome your involvement.

You Make It Happen

Don't be surprised if the young man you are spending time with doesn't have much input initially. While each boy is different, age, shyness, lack of experience in expressing his needs, or feeling uncomfortable being treated as an equal by an adult male will make it hard for him to contribute in the beginning. As the adult, in the early stages of your relationship, you should expect to take most of the initiative for making things happen. Hopefully, you are more organized than the average adolescent and better at planning, and you have more experience in relationships in general. Someday, when the trust between you has evolved and he's gotten more comfortable in the relationship, your young guy will start to have bigger opinions and offer suggestions, and he may even initiate an activity. In the beginning, unlike your adult relationships, expect to do all the work.

Have Reasonable Expectations

In the early stages of your man-making relationship, don't expect things to be perfect, flow smoothly, or be easy. Every boy is different. While everything might unfold nicely, you'll be happier if you plan for a moderately satisfying connection to a younger guy who simply doesn't have great relationship skills. Don't expect your young guy to be conversational, show excitement, gratitude, or even obvious pleasure in your activities at first. He might express his feelings at times, but don't expect it. When there are few signs the young man is actually enjoying the time you share, your work is to just hang in there and trust you are having a positive impact.

Keep in mind that in addition to being a young male, which is plenty of challenge all by itself, the boy you're getting to know will have a complicated life with his family, his own world of personal problems, and a demanding social life with his peers. For the most part, you'll just be an add-on, a cool guy in his life for sure, but just a small part of what, for better or worse, is called his life.

Don't Try to Fix Him

It's important to remember you're not in his life to fix, manage, or take care of your young friend. Many of us had fathers who were primarily disciplinarians. You can be sure this part of yourself will show up and you should be on guard so you don't end up in that role. You may have to work at remembering you're not the boy's parent, teacher, parole officer, therapist, banker, or someone who needs to straighten him out. Unless there is an issue with some aspect of your relationship, you don't have to fix him. Your time with him should be about the upside and fun aspects of being friends. All you have to do is enjoy your time together and leave the hard parts to others. Just being yourself and showing up regularly in his life will have plenty of positive, life-shaping impact.

Keep It Mutual

A man-making relationship should be a mutually rewarding friendship and not something you do for or to a boy. As in all good relationships, once you've gotten to know each other pretty well, you should have a talk about what each of you wants and needs to be comfortable, keep your connection interesting, and make your friendship work. If you don't bring that information into the relationship at some point, one of you will not get your needs met and will eventually go away.

Unless you're following the guidelines of an official mentoring program, the practical things such as where and how often to meet, how long to hang out, and what you're going to do, should all be negotiable and worked out together. Just having a talk about what you each need to make your relationship work is giving the boy a big lesson about how to function in a relationship...another skill he'll use the rest of his life.

Be a Partner in Discovery

As your relationship with a boy unfolds, it's important to treat the young man as a partner in discovery. Instead of just taking him along on the ride of your interests, be teachable yourself. If you can discover some activities he'd enjoy, and then risk doing some of those things, you just might find yourself transported to a completely new world of adventure. I can guarantee you'll experience new sights, sounds, food, movies, and people you wouldn't normally choose for yourself because you'll be experiencing the world from the boy's perspective.

In my man-making relationships with young guys, I've spent more time shooting hoops, playing computer games, listening to rap music, seeing science fiction movies, tossing balls around, and eating "chicken fingers" than I'd ever have experienced on my own. It's precisely because those things are so *not me* that I've loved every minute of each adventure. In following the boy's interests, you'll get to revisit your memories of that time in your life, and explore that era all over again.

In being open to new experiences and willing to experiment with new activities, you are making a large and important statement. You are showing the boy that a man with self-confidence can willingly take on fresh challenges and handle what comes up. Reminders of these lessons are a gift to both yourself and the boy.

Have Regular and Positive Contact

You'll have the most impact in a boy's life when you have regular contact. As a rule, consistency of contact is more important than occasionally doing something spectacular. I try to set up weekly contact, if possible. When you're not able to get together in person, try to call, e-mail, or send a card. It's great to do the big "memory makers," like the Monster Truck Rally or the professional sports game, but it's more important to be in the young man's life often, reliably, and predictably. In the beginning, decide on a schedule that's very comfortable for the two of you, agree on it, and then do everything in your power to honor your commitments.

Remain Optimistic

In all relationships there are ups and downs, and on-and-off days. You should expect some setbacks, disagreements, false starts, and even disappointments. It takes time to get the bugs out, to get to know each other, and to get your partnership working.

It will take time for history and trust to develop between the two of you…maybe a long time. That's why remaining optimistic, especially in the beginning of the relationship, will require an enormous amount of patience. One or the other, or even both of you, may be bringing to the relationship a history of abandonment by some of the men in your lives. As a result, you may experience some very uncomfortable false starts and a lumpy beginning to your friendship. The young man may test your degree of commitment by not returning calls, missing meeting times, and generally being a pain, just to see if you'll hang in there with him. To get through this period, it will help if you make a personal commitment to stay in the relationship, no matter what, for a certain amount of time. Your commitment will be sensed by the boy and eventually trusted. Thirty-eight-year-old Patrick remembers feeling the rock-solid commitment of a man who was supporting him.

> I remember when an important man in my life said
> to me, "There is nothing you can do to make me not love
> you." It was an unbelievably powerful statement to hear
> from a man I held in such high esteem.

Adolescent boys don't trust others easily, and it may take quite a long time for the young male to be relaxed and comfortable with you. A given in most one-on-one man-making relationships is that you won't see many outward signs of the impact you're having. That's why you have to have faith you're making a difference. Know in your heart why *you* are involved so you're not dependent on the boy's feedback for your satisfactions… and then stay optimistic.

You're Not Locked In

It's important to know your relationship with the young man doesn't have to last forever, you're not trapped, and you have an exit if you need it. You don't want to hang in there for a very long time if the relationship isn't a good match, respectful, or fun for you. For some men, knowing they can get out of a commitment to a young man, if necessary, can make it easier to enter a man-making relationship in the first place.

Your connection to the boy can end for many reasons. For example, one of you could move away, one of your lives could get too complicated, or either one of you could lose interest. You could come to the end of your agreed-upon time commitment or one or the other of you could just decide the connection you're trying to build isn't working. Whatever the reason, if it's appropriate *and you've done your best*, you should end the relationship.

When I say end the relationship, I don't mean let the relationship quietly fade off into nothing. When that happens no one knows what's going on and both parties are left with lots of big feelings and questions about their worth and lovability. Too many boys have had the adult males in their lives either not be interested in them at all or, in some way, simply disappear.

Ideally, a good ending is an active process in which you actually get together, say what you feel, and kick around the idea of ending the relationship. You may want to take some time off to think about it and then get back together to talk some more. You can talk about what was good and worked, and what wasn't working. After that process, if it's the right thing to do, make a conscious and *mutual* choice to stop meeting.

Endings, because of the complicated and hard-to-express feelings, are often the hardest part of relationships. That is especially true for a boy with a very limited emotional vocabulary. However, if you do it gently and with respect, it can be a statement of caring, in which you let the boy know what you've valued about him and your time together. Instead of it being more proof he's unloved, or worse unlovable, the ending experience can be something positive and will be another important life lesson for the young man.

There are never any guarantees. Your efforts at building a man-making connection with a young male will take some work and may not be initially rewarding. However, if you hang in there, and your experience is at all similar to that of the many thousands of men who have been in one-on-one man-making relationships, you'll most likely have a lot of fun and maybe make a life-long male friend.

To the world, you may be one person,
but to one person you may be the world.

– Unknown

6

Men In Action

So far, you've learned about seeing, acknowledging, and blessing boys, men in one-man-to-many boys activities, and the different forms of one-on-one, man-making relationships. We've learned about the critical importance of these types of connections and the powerful influences on both men and boys in all these forms of man-making.

However, something else is happening in the masculine universe. As more men are getting directly involved in man-making, they are coming together to create new ways to show up for young males. The result of their concentrated efforts are life-changing for many. Just ahead you'll find descriptions of just some of the ways motivated and boy-literate men are making a difference in both the lives of young males and in their communities.

It's important for you to know the men involved in these activities are regular guys, just like you. Their only qualifications are their clear intentions and strong commitment to support boys on their journey toward a successful manhood. Let's explore just a few of the ways men, acting together, are changing the world.

Community Interventions

What follows are descriptions of two community-based programs in which motivated groups of men gathered around their common intention to take action and make a positive difference in the lives of boys, men, and their communities.

Str8Street

I've always said we don't so much have a young male-driven violence problem in our cities as an epidemic of under-male-nourished boys. Without the boy-civilizing influence of older men in young guys' lives, you are guaranteed to have testosterone-fueled, and out of control, young males running around, trying to be "men," and getting into trouble. There is an often quoted African proverb which in effect says, *If the young men are not initiated into the life of the Village, they will burn it down just to feel the heat.* Today we call that situation a gang problem.

Recently I was part of the launch of an extraordinary program called Str8Street. It's a community intervention program with the goal to reach out to gang-vulnerable young males. In Carson City, Nevada there is a growing presence of mostly white and Hispanic gangs. One young man, named Jose, managed to step out of a gang and gotten himself clean and sober. He then approached The Boys and Girls Clubs of Western Nevada Mentor Center with an idea. He wanted to do something to keep young kids off the streets and out of gangs.

About the same time, the staff of the Mentor Center had heard me speak at a conference on how to get men to show up for young males. We all got connected, had many conversations, and together came up with the idea for Str8Street. The goal of the program is to get a diverse tribe of good men involved in doing things with a multicultural mix of young boys before they are old enough to hear the powerful call into gangs.

For Str8Street's introduction, we invited men from all parts of the community. In attendance were male staff from the Boy's and Girl's Club, parole officers, the sheriff, past gang members, college kids, some young dudes, and many good men from the community. No women were allowed. I did a presentation titled, *Building the Men's Hut: A Conversation about Men, Manhood, and the Boys in Our Village.* The result of that program, simply put, was almost unanimous support for the intentions and goals of the Str8Street program. Many men signed up to participate, community support was enlisted, and a launch date chosen.

The launch event was an overnight campout full of games, adventure, food, and time around the fire. Males of all ages and backgrounds were present, shared in the events, and most importantly, shared their stories and hopes for the future of Str8Street. At the end of the campout, all the participants received a silver dog tag that read Str8Street, marking their participation and the common bond that had been established.

Since the campout, the boys and men have had a wide variety of learning experiences and local adventures. They've learned to shop for groceries and then how to barbeque. They have gone rock climbing, learned how to create and set goals, done some basic car maintenance, explored an art and cultural museum, had CPR training, gone scuba diving in a pool, and played team sports. Each event includes time for going over the rules for the group, a post-event discussion about what was learned, and some casual time learn about what is and is not working in each of the boys' lives. As the program evolves, the boys will have more input into what they want to experience and a chance to demonstrate leadership by running parts of the meetings.

What is so innovative about this program is that good men from all parts of the community are involved. The program keeps men engaged because most of the activities appeal to males of all ages and the time investment is small. In addition to the fun, men get to meet and hang out with new male friends, and experience the satisfaction of making a positive contribution to their community. It also is true that adult male hearts are often profoundly softened by the connection to the young dudes.

Lakes Area Guy's Network - LAGN

The Lakes Area Guys Network (LAGN) was born in 2009 when I went to Brainerd, MN to discuss a group mentoring model for men and young males. I was part of a conversation at the town library with community members and a number of social service agency representatives. Together they expressed concern for the problems many adolescent males were creating in their town. It was the hope of those present that a coordinated effort of some kind could be created to support these young males and to keep them out of trouble.

Their target group was middle school (grades 5-8) with an emphasis on those from single parent families. The idea was to populate the program with boys through referrals from schools, social service agencies, and even law enforcement. They would then take part in activities with good men from the community. It was felt the physical activity, learning, play, connection to good men, fun and positive attention would be good for everyone involved.

Following that meeting, a new community venture was formed, and LAGN's first activities were held in January of 2010. Today, the LAGN has become an official group mentoring project of Kinship Partners, a lakes-area mentoring organization. There is a core group of six men who are responsible for the logistics of the 2-3 activities a month, but LAGN is always recruiting men who are willing to share their interests and skills. Events are usually outdoors (all seasons) and involve fun activities such as kickball, cross country skiing, snow shoeing, broomball, snow tubing, disc golf, football, whiffleball, and fishing (a very popular offering in a "land of lakes").

Could you pull together a small group of motivated men willing to take some small action to positively influence the lives of boys (and men) in your neighborhood or community?

Informal Initiations, Ceremony, and Rites of Passage

Because boys' arrival into manhood is more gradual than their female counterparts, they are more dependent on the world outside themselves to mark important moments on their journey toward manhood. That is why the role of initiations and rites of passage experiences are so critical. Today, men all over the world are conducting initiations, celebrations, and both informal and formal rite of passage experiences for young males.

The scope of these passage experiences includes everything from the "new guy" being welcomed into a team or a profession, novel teen birthday celebrations, and serious, multi-day, rite of passage events. Let's begin increasing your awareness of these transitional experiences by exploring some informal initiations.

Informal Initiations

Informal initiations happen in many different ways, but sometimes you have to look close to see them. For example, you can usually find informal initiations in the trades, on work or athletic teams, in men's clubs, and anywhere the new guy is seeking membership into a male community. Most likely you can remember a time when you were the "new guy" and had to endure some large or small trial to gain full membership into a "tribe" of men.

I remember listening to an old fisherman speaking at the maritime fishing museum on the shore of Lake Superior in Bayfield, Wisconsin. He was describing the seaworthiness of the Lake Superior gill net fishing boat. It had an all-metal construction, an odd whale-like shape, a completely enclosed workspace, and a small coal stove for heat. It was a boat perfectly designed for working the cold and often stormy seas fishermen encounter on the big lake. The old fisherman said they had a special way of initiating the new guys into the profession.

> When we had a fresh young helper on the crew, we'd wait for a good'n stormy day for the "welcome." As part of the tradition, someone would kindly take the new man out for a large and greasy breakfast. Then, when the boat was pitching and rolling in the big water outside the islands and the new guy was below working on the nets, one of us old guys would commence with spitting tobacco juice on the hot stove.
>
> That odor, along with the heating of the wooden floor with its years of accumulated fish gut residue, would raise up a stink you could smell in a fog bank long before you could even hear an engine. This trial by fear, sea, and stink always brought the new guy to his knees, and, of course, increased his respect for us old-timers.

The old fisherman was laughing during the telling of this tale, most likely because he and many generations before him had experienced this uncomfortable initiation. It was a rite of passage ordeal that earned the initiate a degree of acceptance into that world of men. These kinds of informal "initiations" are still common today in many professions.

Adolescent Birthday Celebrations

A perfect opportunity for a ceremony publicly acknowledging a young male's movement toward manhood are his teen birthdays. By the time he's in his teens, a boy is sensing his emerging masculinity and beginning to hunger for something different by way of celebration. Sadly, many boys just get a birthday card with a few bucks in it, and then they and their friends are stuffed in the back of a van and hauled off to an arcade for games and pizza. These actions, or something equally irrelevant, are very poor substitutes for a true passage celebration that can only occur a few times during adolescence.

The teen years, from thirteen to sixteen (depending on the boy), are a time in a boy's life when he is uniquely open to the transformational drama of even a brief ceremony and adult male influences. This is when an informed and motivated man-maker can really make a huge difference in a young guys psyche. Teen birthdays are great opportunities to acknowledge, instruct, and bless a boy on his journey to manhood. It's a natural time to cast the spotlight of positive attention on the adolescent male, to honor his accomplishments, express pride in his person, witness his growing maturity, and elevate him in the eyes of his family and friends.

One great example of how to maximize the man-making potency in a birthday celebration is described in a story from thirty-eight-year-old Patrick.

> To celebrate my son Christopher's thirteenth birthday, with more than a little anxiety I invited some of my male friends and some of my son's male relatives to help me create a "coming-of-age" experience. For this event no women were allowed.
>
> On the appointed day, the men arrived and after some general schmoozing, they made a circle and put Christopher in the center. The men took turns telling stories about themselves, their journey to manhood, and important life lessons they had learned. Some shared scripture passages, and others gave Christopher meaningful but not expensive gifts that symbolized their wishes, hopes, and dreams for him.
>
> Some of the men stepped forward and made verbal commitments of ongoing connection and support to Christopher. Toward the end of the ceremony, I gave my son a ring that was to be an enduring symbol of his mom and my commitment to him, and a constant reminder of our profound love for him.

By inviting his son's male elders to create a coming-of-age ceremony instead of a regular birthday party, Patrick and the other men gave his son an incredible gift. At the end of this powerful experience, Christopher had little doubt he had been recognized and honored as an emerging man. It was clear he was cared for by the men of his tribe, and that he would continue to be supported by those men on his journey to manhood.

If you want to try your hand at an informal ceremony when a young male you know is about to mark some crossing of a line from boyhood in the direction of manhood, consider a simple passage ritual. Birthdays, getting a permit to drive, success on his first hunt or fishing expedition, a first paying job, a relationship break up, graduating high school, just about any important life experience can be worthy of celebration.

You may need parental permission to do something a little special, but it shouldn't be difficult to get. You can simply do it yourself or you can put out the call to older boys and men from the boy's life to show up and honor the young man.

On these occasions, if older males bring a young male into their circle and then engage in the actions of storytelling, talking directly to the boy, lighting a fire (candles), gifting, sharing food, presenting objects and imbuing them with meaning, they are recreating elements of age-old rite of passage ceremonies.

As it has been for thousands of years, the young man at the center of all this attention is not only honored but is guaranteed to feel seriously launched on his journey to manhood. It's also happens to be very good for the masculine souls of the rest of the men participating in the event.

Celebrating a boy in this way, at this time in his life, is high-quality man-making. The important shift for you is to learn to see adolescent birthdays and other important life experiences as opportunities for coming-of-age celebrations. The next step is to accept the fact that you, as an adult male in his tribe, have an opportunity, maybe responsibility, and hopefully the courage to use simple celebrations to help the young man recognize and value his progress toward becoming a man.

> *Boys everywhere have a need for rituals marking their passage to manhood. If society does not provide them, they will inevitably invent their own.*

> – Joseph Campbell
> Mythologist and author

Unfortunately, when it comes to helping mark a boy's movement toward manhood, most men don't realize the importance of these crossings, or have the notion it's men's work to conduct simple ceremonies or honor a boy in these moments. At the same time, we are learning if men don't gather around adolescent males and clearly mark and celebrate their passage into manhood, two things are very likely to happen. First, the boys, feeling biologically driven to express and validate their emerging manhood, will attempt to do it on their own, most often with tragic consequences. A second likely outcome is the boys who feel they never really crossed a line into manhood will become lost men. Men who will forever wander through their lives confused about and searching for a realized masculine identity and potential.

I don't remember any big personal trials as a young man that marked my passage into manhood, but I am still haunted by a memory of a movie titled *A Man Called Horse*, with Richard Harris. In the movie, he played a white man who wanted to be accepted by a tribe of Native Americans and had to prove himself worthy.

He endured a rite of passage that left me breathless. He was led into a huge, dim, and smoky tepee and surrounded by the elders of the tribe. His shirt was stripped off his back and his torso was bare. Two elders tied eagle talons to the ends of two ropes and then the eagle talons were hooked under each of his pectoral muscles. He was then hoisted about three to four feet off the ground. To pass this test, he couldn't jerk around or cry out in pain. He just hung there until he passed out. This was the price of acceptance into the tribe.

Since seeing that movie, I've wondered where is my tribe, and what will I be asked to do to prove myself worthy of their acceptance?

Larry – 47

Formal Rite-of-Passage Programs

For hundreds of years, in cultures all around the world, there have been rite of passage rituals honoring the important transitions in a man's life. In many places, these ancient rituals are still being performed. The rites of passage marking a boy's entrance into manhood are especially powerful, and clearly show a young male where he is in the process of becoming a man. When passage rituals don't occur when they should, or don't take place at all, our communities suffer all the consequences of living with lost men and boys.

Meladona Some, an African spiritual teacher who underwent a forty-day rite of passage in the jungle as a teenager, believes that without rites of passage, a civilization is ill. He says, "When a civilization lacks rites of passage, its soul is sick. The evidence for this sickness is threefold: first, there are no elders; second, the young are violent; third, the adults are bewildered."

> Speaking from traditional definitions, I don't know that I see myself as a man today. I know I am a male. For me to be able to have a defining moment of when I became a man, a rite of passage so to speak, would mean first that I would have to have a good definition (for me) of what a man is, and I don't. No one else gave me that

blessing either. I don't think coming of age necessarily makes a man, but I think our culture would have you believe so.

Phil – 59

Today, formal rite of passage experiences are being offered to young males by many groups of men across the globe. Using ancient rite of passage templates, combined with modern language and experiences, groups of men are refining the elements of this age-old practice for initiating today's men and boys.

What follows are examples of this work from four different groups, from the U.S.A., Australia, New Zealand, and Canada. In each case, these men are re-inventing and then implementing their version of this important work. You can find descriptions of additional formal rite of passage programs on the Man-Making Blog (journeytomanhood.blogspot.com).

> *As for the essential messages of initiation, I have gleaned these from my cross-cultural observations. Somehow, male initiation must communicate the following to the young man:*
> - *Life is hard.*
> - *You are going to die.*
> - *You are not that important.*
> - *You are not in control.*
> - *Your life is not about you.*
>
> – Father Richard Rohr
> From an article titled "Boys to Men"

The Boys to Men Mentoring Network

Before he passed away in 1997, Herb Sigurdson was the head of Boys Town, headquartered in Omaha, Nebraska. Herb's life mission was to support men and youth in building a better world.

The result of that passion is the Boys to Men Mentoring Network (boystomen.org), now in the capable hands of Herb's son, Joe Sigurdson, and his friend and ally, Craig McClain.

Together, Joe and Craig have developed a dramatic, life-changing, weekend initiation experience in which boys, ages twelve to seventeen, are challenged to take a hard look at their lives with the caring support of older men. As a direct result of the many different kinds of challenges the boys face over the weekend, they come to see themselves in new ways. The boys discover their strengths, talents, and other gifts, and they grow more confident. Over the course of the weekend, they also learn to trust themselves, one another, and the men on staff.

During the initiation weekend, the boys interact with positive male role models. They experience a safe place where they can express their feelings, have many opportunities to share their burning issues and questions, *and* get some answers. Along the way, they have a lot of fun and have adventures that are perfectly tailored to an adolescent male.

> *If not us, who will be the men that provide our young boys with guidance, healthy male influences, and positive masculine role models? If not here, where else will they learn how to be a man? If not now, when will they ever learn?*
>
> From the Boys to Men weekend training

To insure the integrity of the weekend experience, all men who want to staff the rite of passage weekend go through background checks and are required to take an intensive, forty-eight-hour training program. In addition to providing men with the skills they need for staffing, the training activities re-sensitize men to the issues, concerns, frustrations, fears, restless energy, and angst that reside in adolescent males. Men also learn an important part of their job description is to simply listen, accept, admire, and bless the boys.

> Gentlemen, I continue to bask in wonder and grati-
> tude at the privilege of this service to young men. I want
> to remind you that these journeymen (graduates) are
> now our brothers. It calls for a shift in the way we men
> deal with them. It means we don't talk down to them, or
> assume we know their thoughts before they've had their
> say. It means when we are with them, they have a say. We
> still set boundaries as mentors, but they will set theirs too
> and those must be respected. We are their loyal allies. We
> are not over-protective. We are their big brothers. We are
> their witnesses. We are their friends. We listen, accept, and
> admire.
>
> – Charlie Borden
> Boys to Men–Minnesota, weekend coordinator

When asked to describe their program in a few words, Craig McClain said, "We are a caring organization, which, with the help of dedicated men who share our concerns about the quality of boys' lives, is changing the world, one boy at a time."

Pathways to Manhood

The Pathways Foundation based in Sydney, Australia, assists teen-agers in making, "the fundamental emotional shift from being a child to becoming a young adult." They do that by providing contemporary, community-based Rites of Passage for boys 13-15, titled Pathways to Manhood, and a similar program for girls 12-15, titled Pathways into Womanhood.

Their very successful and award-winning Pathways to Man-hood program comes from a rich history of experimentation by highly committed individuals arising out of the 1995 Australian and New Zealand Men's Leadership Gathering (ANZMLG). It has been running in communities and schools around Australia since that 1995 beginning.

> "I dream of creating a vehicle, a form, a process for the far children by which they and their generations may honour each other. It must be so beautiful that they won't be able to resist it. It must also be flawed enough that they won't be able to keep their hands off it."

– Don Bowak
Pathways Foundation founding member and Elder

The current Pathways to Manhood approach recognizes all indigenous societies had some form of initiation for their teenagers and there were commonalities in those rituals regardless of where in the world they were held. The Pathways initiations are based on these models. At their camps, they model and teach boys to embody three key values: respect, responsibility, and awareness. They feel the key outcomes of a Pathways camp experience should include:

- strong, long-term relationships between father and son;
- respectful relationships with mothers;
- increase in boys' self-esteem;
- boys taking greater responsibility for their own behavior;
- improved communication and conflict-resolution skills;
- ongoing support for boys to keep their lives 'on track'.

The aim of all Pathways to Manhood initiations is to bring out the full potential of young men and women, and to fill them with hope and inspiration as they look to the future. On their website at pathwaysfoundation.org.au, they state a very worthy goal: "Our aim is to provide every Australian teenage boy and girl with a fun, adventurous, rite of passage transition process into young adulthood."

The power of the Pathways to Manhood program to touch the lives of men and boys is indicated by the following statement from Allan, one of the program's facilitators:

> On one of our first programs, there was a young man of fourteen years. He was surly and resistant, slipping away at every opportunity for a smoke and never making eye contact. By the end of this bush experience he stood tall, looked me in the eye, and had every other youth looking up to him as their natural leader. Six months later he turned up for the next program wanting to assist and be part of the team. This is why I do this work.

TRACKS

In early 2002 a small group of men, Bryan Hansen, Eric Spiekerman, and Jim Horton, sat down to brainstorm what a contemporary rite of passage program for boys in New Zealand might include. Out of that fire of passion, and commitment for the generations to come, the powerful and life-transforming TRACKS program (tracks.net.nz) they have today was born.

The TRACKS program is another great example of what motivated and boy-literate men can create when they understand how much boys and young men need them. At TRACKS they want men to know they can, ". . . make a positive difference just as they are, even with their doubts, anxieties, and concerns."

On their website at tracks.net.nz/public/programmes the description of their retreat-based program says, "Our Rites of Passage events are about exploring what it is to be a man and creating a memorable time that symbolizes transition from boyhood." TRACKS seeks to help boys integrate what they have learned in their retreat experiences into their regular lives when they return home. They say, "After a Rites of Passage event, a young man is invited back into our Young Leaders program to learn more of what it means to be a peer leader, role model, and mentor, not just in our events, but in our society."

At TRACKS, the facilitators are dedicated to enhancing their communities by supporting boys in becoming good young men. They also say that while their events are ". . . focused on boys becoming young men, they are also about young men becoming mature men, and mature men becoming elders."

Young Men's Adventure Weekend - YMAW

One of my favorite rite of passage weekend models for men and boys is the YMAW, or Young Men's Adventure Weekend. For over twenty-one years, the good men who have been producing the YMAW have been taking somewhere between 50 dedicated men and 70 or 80 energetic young males, 12- 17 years-old, off to a gorgeous slice of the Canadian wilderness near Vancouver, British Columbia in Canada. All of the males have the intention of enjoying nature and having an enormous amount of fun, but along the way, the young guys learn some very important lessons about manhood.

Brad Leslie, one of the founders of YMAW, says, "I am always amazed by the change in the young men in just 48 hours. So many of them go from shy, unsure, and rebellious when they come in on Friday evening, to standing tall, confident, making eye contact and firm handshakes when they leave. It is always inspiring for me."

The YMAW vision statement reads, "Creating healthy communities by building strong, spirited young men who will become great husbands, fathers, and leaders." Doesn't that straighten your masculine spine and make you want to help them?

The YMAW is a deeply transformational and often life-changing experience for all the males involved. On the YMAW website (ymaw.com) you can learn more about this grand and very male experience, see some highly inspirational video, and learn how you might become an "outlander" staff man on their weekend if you're willing to travel.

• • • • •

The Man-Making Blog (journeytomanhood.blogspot.com) has a growing list of rite of passage organizations and programs. You'll also find many other examples of men working together to create informal initiations, community service projects, and other men-in-action programs. Wherever in the world these programs occur, the men involved will tell you that every male who participates, regardless of his age, is powerfully transformed by these experiences. If you are interested in starting or participating in similar programs, contact me via the Man-Making Website, at man-making.com, and I'll help you find a way to get involved.

7

Answering the Man-Making Call

My Man-Making Story

Since that happy day when I heard the call to man-making, my connection to boys, men, and my life has never been the same. Just like this book, I am also a work in progress. Today, I'm directly involved with a half-dozen adolescent males through informal/ natural mentoring relationships. I volunteer with two organizations whose stated purpose is to initiate young males and then do group mentoring to help move them toward a positive manhood. I sponsor and participate in events that include men and boys. I have repositioned my speaking, consulting, and writing to be in service to this cause. Finally, I now have men friends and heroes from all over the world who, in many different ways, are stepping up as man-makers for young males.

I am not bragging. I am simply telling you what has unfolded, *naturally*, in my life as I responded to the man-making call I heard. While I am humbled by the contributions to this work by so many good men, I, too, have become committed to doing what I can to help and support boys, adolescent males, and the men I encounter, on our collective journey toward manhood. I can say that my masculine esteem is growing and I feel I am a better man as a result of my involvement. I want the same for you and the men and boys around you.

Profile of a Man-Maker

When I asked contributors to this book about the ways they are engaged with the boys in their communities, one of the men really caught my attention. Jon H. is a man who takes his man-making capacity and responsibility very much to heart. I want to hold him up as a powerful example of an aware, male-literate, loving, compassionate, engaged, and action-oriented man-maker. What follows is his list of responses to the question, "What do you do with and for young boys in your community?"

- Listen and hear what they are saying.
- Encourage them to be in my house and yard.
- Support and encourage them.
- Set boundaries.
- Participate in Cub Scouts and Boy Scouts.
- Admit my mistakes.
- Volunteer in a school reading program that is mostly boys.
- Staff Boys-to-Men initiation weekends.
- Assure young males with safety pins in their noses that I am not disturbed by them and do not judge them.
- Volunteer as a Guardian Ad Litem (court advocate) for young men.
- Organize community support for, and staff, a Father and Son special event.
- Volunteer in an alternative school as anger management group facilitator.
- Chair the "Festival of Fathers" event.
- Keep them in my heart and mind all the time.

Jon is one of my personal heroes. Few men I know have his level of commitment, or more interaction with men and boys.

How would your life be different today if you had been sur-rounded by men like Jon when you were an adolescent? Just think about the many ways life for young males would change for the better if every man in your community had even a small degree of Jon's commitment to men, boys, and man-making.

Answering the Call

As this edition of *Man-Making—Men Helping Boys on Their Journey to Manhood* is published, the world seems to be increas-ingly aware of the many challenges facing our young males. There have been articles on the "boy crisis" regularly appearing in magazines and newspapers. Documentary productions on the topic are showing up on television and in films, and new research seems to be continuously emerging. On the Man-Making Blog (journeytomanhood.blogspot.com) and Man-Making Website (man-making.com), I will continue do my best to keep you apprised of current research, and relevant programs, websites, books, and resources. I'll continue to profile men's stories, and hold up great man-making role models for emulation.

What will *not* change, however, is how much the boys in *your* community need *you* to get involved in man-making. I have heard the call to action and this book is one of the ways I can do some-thing to support you and the young males who are our future. My deepest wish is that you find it in your heart to respond to the call you hear, and find some large or small way to make a difference in the lives of young males around you.

There is no question there is a desperate need for men, *you*, to step into man-making activities and that a multitude of opportunities are waiting. I believe all men who hear this call to action, however faintly, must accept this life-giving and life-sav-ing responsibility and take action. No matter how imperfect you feel your actions might be, they will be far better than the abandonment boys are currently experiencing. I believe men must act now, for the sake of the boys around them who are crying out for their influence and guidance, for their communities, and to fully realize their full masculine potential.

You wouldn't be reading this if you hadn't heard the ancient call to man-making, and were, to some degree, willing to face that challenge. The only remaining question is when will you step out on this part of *your* journey to manhood? Your mature masculinity and the boys are waiting. Thank you for caring about men and boys, and my blessings on your intentions.

References

In addition to these books, a long list of additional books, films, and helpful websites can be found in the Resources section of the Man-Making Website at man-making.com.

Garbarino, James. 1999. *Lost Boys: Why Our Sons Turn Violent and How We Can Save Them*. New York: Anchor Books.

Golding, William. 1959. *The Lord of the Flies*. New York: Perigee Trade.

Gurian, Michael. 1997. *The Wonder of Boys*. New York: Putnam.

Gurian, Michael, and Kathy Stevens. 2005. *The Minds of Boys*. San Francisco: Jossey-Bass.

Kipnis, Aaron. 1999. *Angry Young Men: How Parents, Teachers, and Counselors Can Help "Bad Boys" Become Good Men*. San Francisco: Jossey-Bass.

Moore, Robert L., and Douglas Gillette. 1991. *King, Warrior, Magician, Lover: Rediscovering the Archetypes of the Mature Masculine*. New York: HarperCollins.

Pollack, William S. 1999 -2004. *Real Boys: Rescuing Our Sons from the Myths of Boyhood*. New York: Owl Books.

Price, Geoff. 2006. *Puberty Boy*. Crows Nest, New South Wales: Allen & Unwin.

Thompson, Michael, and Dan Kindlon. 2000. *Raising Cain: Protecting the Emotional Life of Boys*. New York: Ballantine Books.

Towle, Tom Owen. 1988. *New Men–Deeper Hungers*. Carmel, California: SunInk Publications.

Williamson, Marianne. 1992. *A Return to Love: Reflections on the Principles of A Course in Miracles*. New York: HarperCollins.

About the Author

Earl Hipp describes himself as a man who was under-fathered and under-male-mentored in adolescence. He was a man who was "left with the women and children to figure out manhood on his own." Since that time, he has learned a lot about manhood and the making of men.

From 1982 until the present, Earl has consistently been involved with groups and organizations that focus on men's issues and development. He has led and participated in rite of passage initiation experiences for young males. He speaks to and consults with groups and organizations who are trying to call men into service to boys. He consults with communities in the development of violence prevention programs and other alternatives to gangs for young males. As a direct result of his interest in mens' and boys' issues, he has relationships with young men who have been incarcerated, he maintains many ongoing man-making relationships, and sponsors boys-and-men activities.

Today, Earl's driving passion is to do what he can to ensure fewer boys and men will be left to wander alone in the dangerous never-never land between boyhood and manhood. His goal is to inspire men to turn their natural man-making skills into action. His vision is that someday all young males will be surrounded by good men who will intentionally launch, and then support them on their journey into manhood.

Earl Hipp is an author, publisher, speaker, organizational advisor, and community consultant. He has written seven books about and for adolescents, which together have sold more than a half-million copies. Since 2004, Earl has published the Man-Making

Blog (journeytomanhood.blogspot.com). On the blog he discusses the topics related to manhood, male culture, mentoring, and rites of passage. The blog also showcases model programs, relevant films, books, and related sources.

Earl Hipp lives with his wife, Gwen Barker, spending summers in Minneapolis, Minnesota, and winters in Tucson, Arizona. Earl enjoys time with his family and friends of all ages. Earl loves to hike in the mountains, play at the ocean, and travel to beautiful places. He also enjoys sitting quietly, a good laugh, feeling gratitude, and enjoying a good cup of coffee.

Contacting the Author

I enjoy hearing from my readers. I want to hear about your man-making success stories, challenges, and discoveries. I want to know about good man-making programs, men who are great role models, important books related to this topic, or anything else you feel I should know. You can contact me via the Man-Making Website at man-making.com.

Ordering Information

To order additional copies of the *Man-Making* book, find e-book editions, and learn about the special reports and publications on this topic, visit the Man-Making Website at man-making.com.

Earl's books for young people are on themes such as coping with the stresses in their lives, moving through grief and loss, and understanding the violence in our communities. You can learn about these books at the man-making.com website.

Thank You

I recognize you are the kind of man who cares enough about boys to take the time and energy to read this book. I honor you for your open heart, your ability to see that boys need your involvement, and for simply *considering* what you might do to help a boy or boys.

Because of who you are, I'm sure you are already having impact somewhere. I'm excited about the additional gifts you'll bring to a boy or boys around you when you step into action. From one man to another, thank you for being the kind of man you are, and for caring about boys. I am *already* very proud of you.

– Earl Hipp

CPSIA information can be obtained at www.ICGtesting.com
Printed in the USA
BVOW08s1035301213

340478BV00001B/157/P